Guajira, the Cuba girl

ZITA AROCHA

AN INLANDIA INSTITUTE PUBLICATION

RIVERSIDE, CALIFORNIA

Guajira, the Cuba girl
Copyright © 2024 by Zita Arocha
ISBN: 978-1-955969-23-9 (paperback)
ISBN: 978-1-955969-24-6 (ebook)

Author's Note: Some names have been changed or abbreviated to protect privacy.

Cover art:
Book design and layout: Mark Givens
Publications Coordinator & editor: Maria Fernanda Vidaurrazaga

Library of Congress Cataloging-in-Publication Data
Names: Arocha, Zita, author.
Title: Guajira, the Cuba girl / by Zita Arocha.
Description: First edition. | Riverside, California : Inlandia Institute, [2024] | Summary: "On the eve of leaving Cuba for Florida, a four-year-old girl promises her dying grandfather to return to her birthplace. That night an intruder sexually assaults her. As she adapts to her new American reality, she suffers distressing physical and emotional symptoms. Convinced that her daughter is possessed, her mother takes her to a Santeria priest for a cure. Years later, she returns to her homeland as a journalist, becomes entrapped in the game of espionage between Cuba and the U.S., suffers a devastating betrayal, and learns family secrets. Disillusioned by the experience, she embarks on a spiritual journey that leads to reconciliation, forgiveness, and a return to wholeness"-- Provided by publisher.
Identifiers: LCCN 2023049909 (print) | LCCN 2023049910 (ebook) | ISBN 9781955969239 (paperback) | ISBN 9781955969246 (ebook)
Subjects: LCSH: Arocha, Zita. | Women journalists--United States--Biography. | Cuban Americans--Biography.
Classification: LCC PN4874.A575 G83 2024 (print) | LCC PN4874.A575 (ebook) | DDC 070.92--dc23/eng/20231226
LC record available at https://lccn.loc.gov/2023049909
LC ebook record available at https://lccn.loc.gov/2023049910

Published by Inlandia Institute
Riverside, California
www.InlandiaInstitute.org
First Edition

Guajira, the Cuba girl

Zita Arocha

"Only the self shelters the self. What shelter could there be outside the self."

—The Dhammapada.

"Exile is the unhealable rift forced between a human being and a native place, between the self and its true home."

—Edward Said, Reflections on life in exile

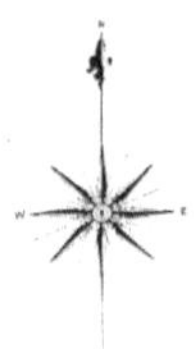

INSURANCE MAPS of TAMPA
INCLUDING
WEST TAMPA.
YBOR CITY,
PORT TAMPA CITY and PORT TAMPA.
FLORIDA
SANBORN-PERRIS MAP CO. Limited
115 Broadway, New York
SCALE 50 FT TO AN INCH
JUNE 1899
Copyright 1899 by the Sanborn-Perris Map Co. Limited

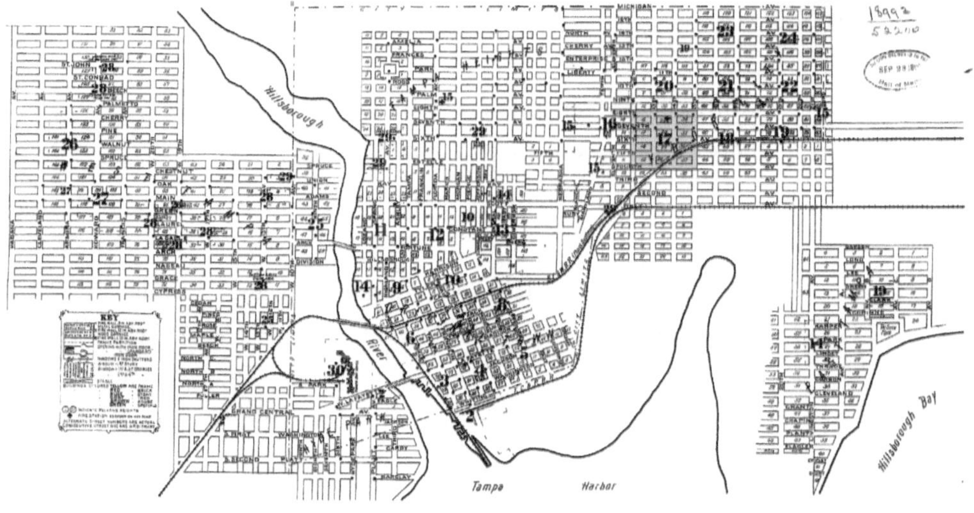

Population 30000. Prevailing Winds N.W. & S.W.
WATER FACILITIES
FIRE DEPARTMENT
West Tampa Water Works
West Tampa to have volunteer hose company
Grades level
Street very sand. Paved streets shown in color on key map.
KEY
Hillsborough
River
Tampa Harbor
Hillsborough Bay
MICHIGAN
AMELIA
FRANCES
NORTH
CHERRY
ENTERPRISE
LIBERTY
ST. JOHN
ST. CONRAD
PALMETTO
CHERRY
PINE
WALNUT
SPRUCE
CHESTNUT
OAK
MAIN
LAUREL
ARCH
NASSAU
GRACE
CYPRESS
DIVISION
POLK
GRAND CENTRAL
WASHINGTON
SECOND
BARLOW
HARPER
LINSEY
CLEVELAND
GRANT
GARFIELD
PLANT

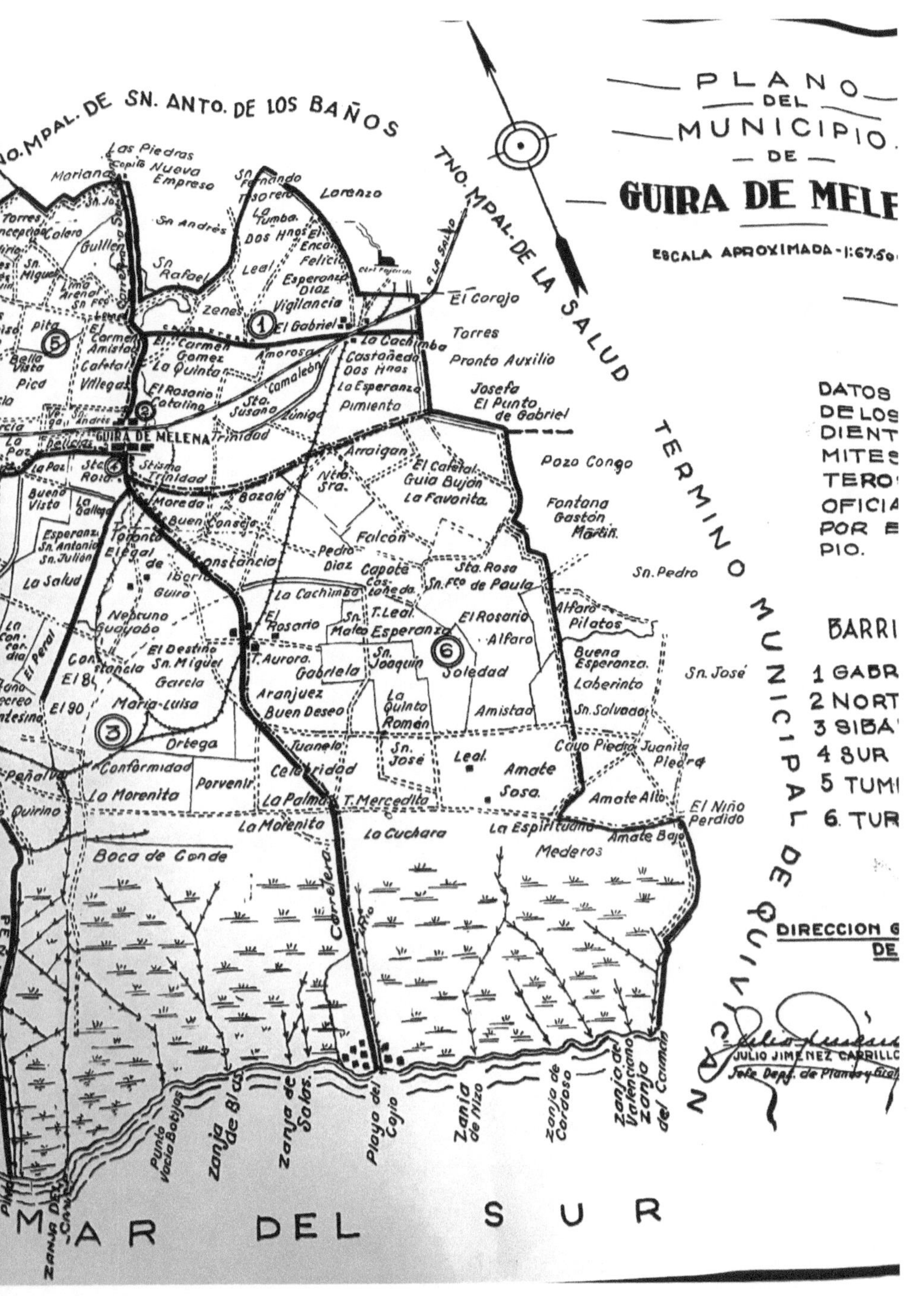
PLANO
DEL
MUNICIPIO.
— DE —
GUIRA DE MELE
ESCALA APROXIMADA - 1:67.50

NO.MPAL. DE SN. ANTO. DE LOS BAÑOS
TNO. MPAL. DE LA SALUD
TERMINO MUNICIPAL DE QUIVICAN

DATOS
DE LOS
DIENT
MITES
TERO
OFICIA
POR E
PIO.

BARRI
1 GABR
2 NORT
3 SIBA
4 SUR
5 TUMI
6. TUR

DIRECCION G
DE

JULIO JIMENEZ CARRILLO
Jefe Dept. de Planos y Gra

Las Piedras
Mariana
Copita Nueva Empresa
Sn. Fernando
Tesorero
Lorenzo
Torres
Concepcion Calero
San José
Guillen
Sn. Andrés
La Tumba
Dos Hnos. El
Encal
Felicia
Sn. Miguel
Sn. Rafael
Leal
Esperanza Díaz
Vigilancia
El Corojo
Lima
Arenal Sn. Feo.
Zenes
El Gabriel
Torres
pita
El
Carmen Amistad
Gómez
El Carmen
Amorosa
La Cachimba
Castañeda
Dos Hnos
Pronto Auxilio
Bella Vista
Cafetal
La Quinta
Camaleón
La Esperanza
Josefa
El Punto de Gabriel
Pica
Villegas
El Rosario
Catalina
Sta. Susana
Zúñiga
Pimienta
Vega Andrés
GUIRA DE MELENA
Trinidad
Pozo Congo
La Paz
Stsma. Trinidad
Arraigan
El Cafetal
Guía Bujón
La Favorita
Fontana Gastón Martín
La Paz
Sta. Rosa
Niño Sra.
Buena Vista
La Gallega
Moreda
Bazala
Falcón
Esperanza Sn. Antonio
Sn. Julián
Toronto
El Gal
Buen Conseja
Pedro Díaz
Capote
Casta neda
Sta. Rosa
Sn. Fco. de Paula
Sn. Pedro
La Salud
de
Constancia
Iberia
La Cachimba
Guira
El Rosario
Sn. Mala Esperanza
T. Leal.
El Rosario
Alfaro Pilatos
La Concordia
Neptuno
Guayabo
El Destino
Sn. Miguel
T. Aurora.
Sn. Joaquín
Alfaro
Buena Esperanza.
Sn. José
El Peral
Constancia
García
Gabriela
Soledad
Laberinto
E 184
Aranjuez
Amistad
Sn. Salvador
recreo
E 190
María-Luisa
Buen Deseo
Antesina
La Quinta Román
Cayo Piedra
Juanita Piedra
Ortega
Juanelo
Sn. José
Leal.
Amate Sosa
Peñalva
Conformidad
Porvenir
Celebridad
Amate Alto
Lo Morenita
La Palma T. Merceditas
El Niño Perdido
Quirino
La Morenita
La Cuchara
La Espirituana
Amate Bajo
Boca de Conde
Mederos
PENA
Punto Vacía Botijas
Zanja de Blanc
Zanja de Solas.
Playa del Cojío
Zanja de Nizo
Zanja de Cordoso
Zanja del Valenciano Zanja del Camán
Zanja del Carm
Carretera
Rio
MAR   DEL   SUR

CONTENTS

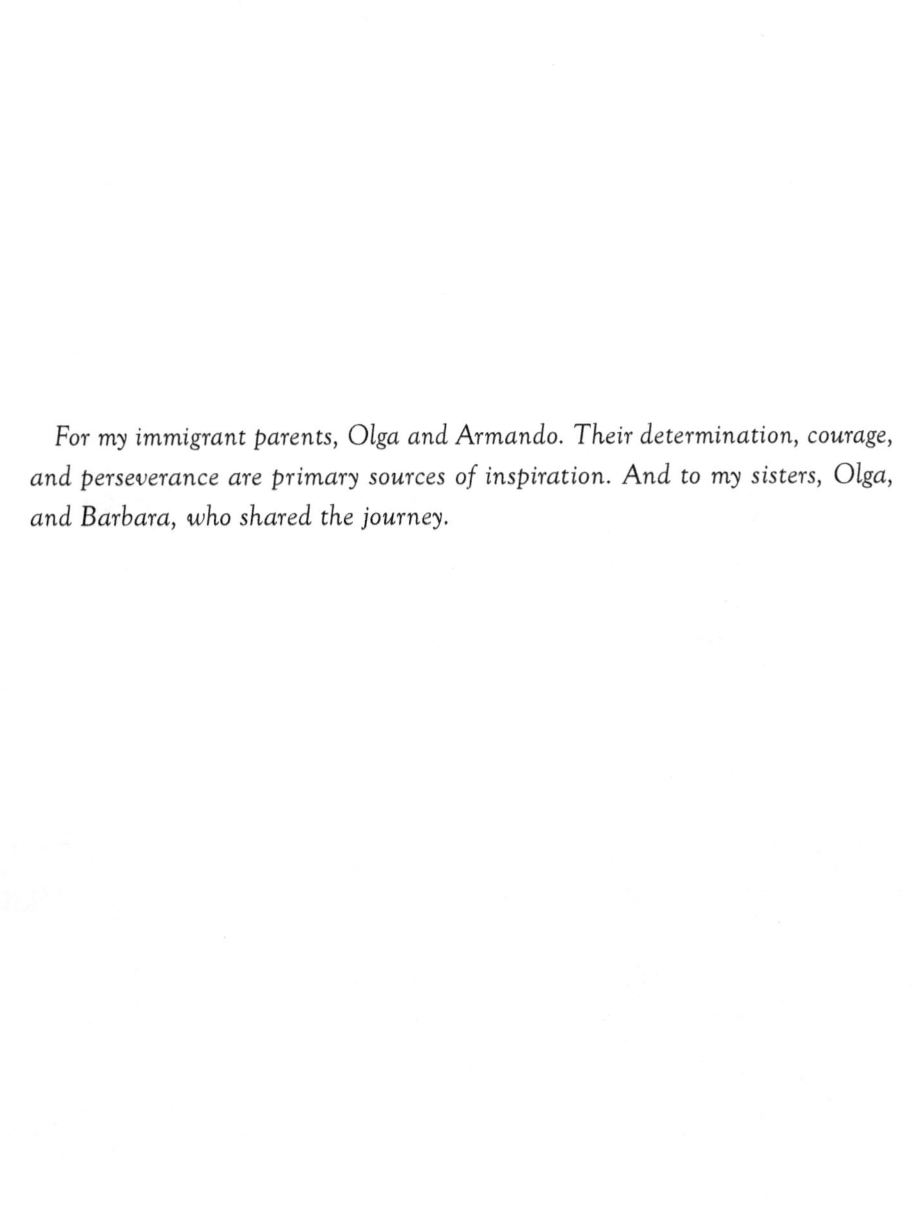

For my immigrant parents, Olga and Armando. Their determination, courage, and perseverance are primary sources of inspiration. And to my sisters, Olga, and Barbara, who shared the journey.

Guajiro: The term may originate from the slaves brought to Cuba from Venezuela in the XVI century... The inhabitants of the Cuban countryside do not like to be called *guajiro* because the term carries a pejorative connotation of rusticity... In the past, *guajiro* was applied to whites (who resided in the countryside) and not to blacks because they were slaves, but following their emancipation, they, too, became *guajiro*.

Excerpted from *Nuevo Catauro de Cubanisms*, by Fernando Ortiz, published in Habana, Cuba, 1985.

Tara Mandala
Pagosa Springs, Colorado
July 2010

PROLOGUE

The flames have died, and all that remains of David, my drum teacher, are bits of bone, some teeth, and slivers of nail burrowed in embers and gray ash. Death intrudes even here.

A few weeks ago, I arrived at this remote Buddhist retreat center cradled like a freshwater pearl inside a Southern Colorado forest. My hybrid green Camry was crammed with sheets, towels, a solar power collector, and soft bags of dried and canned food to last a month. The cabin has no electricity or running water. An outhouse stands perched like a king's crown on a small protruding hill seventy-five feet from my front door. The plan was to use the time here to complete a memoir, keep a diary, meditate, and engage in Buddhist practices, including an esoteric one called "Feeding your Demons." Instead, death has interrupted this rare gift to me—four weeks of absolute solitude and silence—and resurrected memories of other closer deaths and a homeland lost long ago.

I am edgy as I sit cross-legged in a circle with other purple-robed Buddhist practitioners on a rocky stretch of ground ten feet from David's conflagration and watch as dying embers consume what's left of his body behind a rectangle of yellow silk curtains. We chant and sing and play our two-sided Chod drums. Our practice will guide his spirit through the intermediate after-death state of Bardo and help him reach enlightenment rather than return as another suffering being or an animal or insect.

At age 54, lean and rangy as a Texas cowboy—David was an artist, dancer, and builder with no apparent signs of illness—he died in his sleep at home a day ago, perhaps from a brain aneurysm or heart attack.

His wife, Lama Tsultrim, a former nun in Tibet, had spent the night in meditation down the hill at the ornate temple David designed and built. A housekeeper found his inert body in the bedroom of their house the following morning. A muscular young woman called Mountain, who brought me food and water when I needed them, rapped sharply on the door of my one-room cabin named Ratna, which means wish-fulfilling jewel, as I meditated in lotus posture within a patch of sunlight on the cracked cement floor.

"David's dead," she said, her voice trembling as she stared at the criss-cross of cracks and masking tape I'd used on the floor.

"What?" a voice shrieked inside my head, thoughts and heart racing as I recalled my husband David, who was at home with our three dogs.

"David? David. Dead?" I blurted. Sensing my alarm, Mountain clarified she had meant Lama's husband and provided brief details of his death.

After she had gone, I sighed, rushed outside, and stood rigid as an arrow, barely breathing, beneath two giant oaks—one healthy, the other scarred and blackened by lightning. The trees overlooked a glistening green meadow that reminded me of the ocean beyond the malecón in Havana harbor.

"Why?" I yelled out. I listened for a few minutes to the rustling leaves and cawing of crows circling the treetops.

When there was no response to this question, I shouted out more questions to Buddha, Jesus, the universe—whoever was out there.

"Why here, why now?" I listened as my echo cascaded down the mountain and faded into nothingness. I stayed silent and listened to the muted sounds of the still forest until sunset.

Later, as I prepared for bed, I realized David's unexpected death has resurrected memories of other losses. The most wrenching was to leave the topography of my land, close-knit family, and Cuban culture when I was four. Five weeks before boarding a plane in Havana bound for our new home in Florida and waving goodbye to our extended family from behind a smudged plate-glass window at Rancho Boyeros airport, I witnessed my grandfather's death as I stood at his bedside, observing as he gasped his last breaths.

I was his favorite granddaughter, he liked to brag. As was the custom then, Mom permitted him to name me after Zita, an Italian Catholic saint whose name appeared above the morning newspaper headlines the day I was born.

Before taking a last breath through smoke-ravaged lungs, *abuelo* Simon extracted a promise from my mother and me as we sobbed by his bedside: *Don't forget us*, he wheezed. *Regresen*, return.

Later that night, someone assaulted me as I slept a few yards from my grandfather's inert body, which had been laid out on a table beneath a picture of a much younger Simon standing beside a Royal Palm, unsmiling in his wide-brimmed police cap, his back stiff as the starched button-decorated uniform he wore. I still have a fear of dying in my sleep.

Over six decades, I have returned to Cuba often to fulfill the burdensome promise to abuelo, who, despite his strict character and 19th-century machismo, allowed me to sip thick sugary coffee from his miniature cup and play dominos with him and his cronies at the dining table on weekend afternoons. He taught me to count the white dots on the obsidian rectangles as I sat beside him, although I hadn't yet learned to read or write. The counting lesson gave me a heads up in Mrs. Moore's first-grade class at West Tampa Elementary when I was learning to add and subtract using pennies, nickels, dimes, and quarters and wanted to impress my blonde, blue-eyed teacher from Ohio. *Gracias abuelo*. Thank you, grandfather.

Yet, the promise I made to return is a curse. No matter how hard I try to forget her, Cuba keeps calling. I've returned to my homeland many times to reconnect with my dwindling family of origin: as a journalist, as a college teacher, alone, with students, with my husband and stepdaughter, and with my parents. Each time I visit, I think I've said a final goodbye, *adios*, to Cuba. No matter the number of trips home and betrayals by family and others, Cuba beckons like a seductive streetwalker; the moment I board the plane for the return trip to Tampa, Washington, or El Paso—places I've lived and worked—I start to plan my next trip.

As an infant, my mother pinned a small azabache stone in the shape of a hand on my cotton robe as protection against harm. In my country, the Afro-Cuban religion of Santeria is practiced widely—it's said to be more popular than the prevailing Catholicism. Santeria deities, called Orishas, are believed to shower practitioners with blessings and guidance but sometimes use charms and spells to cause harm. The azabache, a shiny black stone originally from Spain, is believed to protect children from the harmful intentions of jealous strangers and ill-wishing friends.

Although I'm not superstitious, and the azabache I wore as a child disappeared long ago, I keep a replica—bought at a street market in Panama—next to my desktop computer. It reminds me of home and protects against writer's block. Other mementos and talismans also elicit childhood memories of home. Three miniature dwarfs sit beside a black-and-white photo of me on my fourth birthday, standing next to a two-tiered birthday cake topped by a plastic set of Snow White and the seven dwarfs. I found three dwarfs inside my mother's dresser drawer when my sister and I were cleaning out her home to move her to a nursing home. The rest were lost along the way. Another precious token is a plastic film canister filled with red dirt. The dirt is from my family's yard in Guira de Melena, a farming village an hour's drive from Havana known for rich red clay that leaves permanent stains on clothes no matter how hard you scrub. The container sits on a bookshelf in my hallway, along with numerous books about Cuba and other sentimental paraphernalia —including a pilfered coffee cup from the famous Hotel Nacional and a baseball that says Cuba.

Cousins presently inhabit my long-dead grandparent's house on Mercedes

Street—the name replaced by a number after the 1959 revolution. They have modernized the thatched-roof leaky wood frame home I remember from childhood with scarce black-market goods. A bathroom with indoor plumbing has replaced the outhouse, and the floors, previously packed with mud and lye, are easy-to-mop concrete. Some of my relatives were born in this house, and a few have died there. A short stroll away is the town cemetery where my grandparents, aunts, and uncles, on both sides, lie stacked on top of one another to save *pesos* and space.

A few years after we resettled in Tampa, Florida, my grandmother Matilde died in the family home; years later, her eldest daughter, my tia Zoraida, took her last breath in a closet-size room on the tiny bed where she was born and gave birth to two children. As she died, my aunt wore Adidas tennis shoes, a gift from my mother. After a long and unhappy life, she wanted to be ready for the quick jog to *paraíso*, which in her imagination would look like the gold-paved streets, lush parks, and jam-packed store shelves of the *uni des stay*, as Mami calls our new country.

No hay mal que por bien no venga goes a popular Cuban expression. Here we have a similar saying: when bad things happen, they happen for a reason.

My drum teacher's unexpected death feels propitious, although I am unsure how. Perhaps it is a necessary jolt to finish a memoir of Cuba I started long ago and to exorcise some demons.

One is my native ground, Cuba, a fickle lover who betrayed me. *Me quiere y no me quiere.* She loves me; she loves me not. I can't let her go, but I need to. It is time.

CHAPTER 1

GUAJIRA, THE RHYTHM CALLS YOU
GUAJIRA, EL SON TE LLAMA

Havana, May 2014

I spot the security agent as I slip into the back of the snaking immigration line at Rancho Boyeros Airport, the pre-revolutionary name for Jose Martí Airport. He is lean with a thin mustache, wears a pressed guayabera, and resembles a younger version of my 84-year-old dad in Florida. He eyes me from his perch against the back wall of the hangar-style building. I pretend not to notice when he leaps toward me across the beige linoleum like a feline after a jutía.

"Qué haces aquí?" he barks, leaning forward, his sculpted nose almost brushing against mine. Why are you here?

I've arrived in my homeland with my husband, David, from El Paso after a one-night layover in Cancun. I am exhausted and hungry, and the heel of my right foot throbs from a gash inflicted during an improvised pedicure the night before.

"Why are you here?" he demands again. I am taken aback by his urgent tone and the implication in his voice: I do not belong.

On this one of many return trips to Cuba over three decades, I arrived to visit what's left of the family, an aging aunt on my father's side and a cousin on my mother's. This is David's first trip to the island. We plan to do research for books we are writing — mine a childhood memoir, David's a thriller about Miami and Central America. On past trips to the island, I combined reporting or teaching assignments with visits to see relatives in Guira, where I was born. This trip is personal. One reason is to fulfill a grandfather's dying wish that I return and not forget my family. The other is discovering who assaulted me the night he died a few weeks before we immigrated to Florida. All I recollect of the traumatic experience are sensory scraps—right arm pinned to the bed, face pressed hard into a pillow, the metallic smell of alcohol on somebody's breath. I never saw a face. Lingering emotional and physical traces of the late-night attack and the burdensome promise to Abuelo when I was four are curses I want to exorcise.

I search for my husband, halfway down a different snaking line, chugging along like a fast-moving train. His eyes, beneath his navy baseball cap, are focused like a drill on reaching the agent checking passports. I think about waving, calling out, but he's rushing away from where this stranger from *Seguridad Cubana*, Cuban Security, has stopped me in my Teva tracks. The last thing I want is a scene in this waiting room.

I swallow hard and point at the rolling Samsonite briefcase at my feet, stuffed with my Mac laptop, pens and pencils, paperclips, a cheap video recorder, a Canon digital camera, notebooks, and a white plastic ring binder filled with over thirty pages of official U.S. documents, including a license from the U.S. Treasury Department and a detailed itinerary of the places I plan to visit. Anticipating problems, I've come prepared to make my case for entry, designed to overcome obstacles I know either government might use to block my travel to the Communist country and to assuage what David calls my lifelong paranoia that concocts cloak-and-dagger conspiracies about anything having to do with my complex birthplace.

The abrupt stop at Paradise's doorstep is unnerving and reminds me of the pigeons that break their necks when they smash into the open windows of my adobe-walled home, having mistaken the green reflection in the glass for the branches of a tree. This watchman, this impediment, is temporary, I repeat to myself like a mantra.

"I'm here to do research," I say in as steady a voice as I can manage. The man's bushy eyebrows quiver above his coffee-colored eyes. His dark mustache switches. Mistake, I catch myself. I've used the Spanish verb for research, *investigar*, a dangerous notion in a totalitarian country.

"What are you investigating?" he demands, his eyes boring into mine like four-inch nails.

"Jose Martí," I say, glancing at my red toes on the beige terrazzo floor. The moment I pronounce the name of Cuba's revolutionary hero and founding father, I feel a sharp stab in my right heel, and suddenly the previous night's dream flashes through my mind—I'm hooked like a fish, the fishhook attached to my womb, and someone is yanking it. It hurts, and I need to remove it.

Shit, I think. You don't go to Cuba to investigate a man the Communists consider their foremost patriot and father of the homeland, a martyr cut down by Spanish guns when he rode a white steed into battle at the start of the Independence War.

"What I mean is I'm working on a novel about Martí," I stammer.

This is a half-truth; I am primarily collecting information for a memoir and have a half-formed idea for a novel about Martí's time in Tampa, where I grew up after leaving Cuba.

"El proser," he interjects and nods as if trying to decide what to do with this blue-eyed gringa-looking woman who speaks Spanish like a native and clutches a U.S. passport like a lucky rabbit's foot.

Level with him, I think, and launch into a rapid-fire explanation of my background and motivation.

I was born in Cuba in 1952, left with my parents in 1957; dad was a poor guajiro—this to differentiate us from the once-rich property owners who fled after Castro came to power—*we still have family on the island. I teach at a university in Texas and am writing a book,* I say, stopping to catch my breath.

"Where's your Cuban passport?" he growls.

"No tengo. I don't have one."

"Follow me," the security man orders, and I hobble behind him, my hope of entry deflating like a birthday balloon after the party.

"Coño," I curse the uniquely Cuban expletive under my breath and follow him to a roped-off area, where several men and women in beige uniforms huddle in a circle like birds pecking at worms.

After he disappears down a corridor, one of the uniformed women edges toward me and asks—again, this time politely—why I am here, what I am writing about, and what places I plan to visit. I fumble with the zipper of my briefcase, reach inside, and retrieve the five-inch white binder with my dated and stamped U.S. travel license, a letter signed by my graduate advisor at the university, and a detailed itinerary that includes the Cuban National Library, the house where Martí was born, the Palace of the Revolution and the famously ornate Colón Cemetery in the city center. She seems uninterested as I flip through the pages and say in a confident tone: "This is why I am here."

David, a Costa Rican-born U.S. citizen, has breezed through immigration and customs lines and retrieved his rolling red suitcase. He approaches the cordoned area where I am being held hostage.

"She's my wife," he says, pointing at me.

One woman lifts the rope so he can join me inside the circle.

"What's going on?" he whispers, and I explain.

"Don't lose your temper," he says close to my ear and touches my elbow. He's seen me tangle with Mexican Customs agents in Ciudad Juarez over a permit to drive my car into the country, arguing nose-to-nose with a burly El Paso tow-truck driver as he tried to strap chains on the tires of my Toyota, shooting a bird at an aggressive driver through the streets of Old San Juan. I agree; best stay calm.

Fifteen minutes later, a distinguished gray-haired man wearing a dark jacket in his fifties strides toward us down a long corridor.

"How much cash have you brought?"

Two thousand dollars—U.S.

"Do you have credit cards?"

Yes.

"Which ones?"

Visa and American Express.

I know they're useless in Cuba, but I've brought them for our stopover in Cancun.

"What's the name of the hotel where you will stay?"

Hotel Vedado in Central Havana.

"What are the names and addresses of your family members in Cuba?"

I give him the name of my cousin Mirta and her address in Guira de Melena, the house where my mother was raised, my grandfather and grandmother died, and where Mirta's mother, my tia Zoraida, lived her entire married life until she died in her 80s. Mirta shares the tiny house with her remaining twin son, her son's wife, and their three young daughters.

"Teléfono?" the man inquires.

My cousin does not own a telephone, I explain. I reach her by calling a neighbor who lives a few blocks away, who then sends her son to let Mirta know she has a *llamada*, a call from the U.S.

Some Cubans with phones make a little extra money by charging neighbors for making and receiving phone calls. This neighbor doesn't charge my cousin.

After answering a few more questions and—again—showing him the contents of my thick binder, he disappears down the cavernous corridor, leaving me alone because the other security guards have disappeared, and David waits on a nearby bench.

It's almost midnight, two hours since my injured foot touched Cuban soil. I am mentally preparing for the next flight home.

Suddenly, a third man in a dark jacket approaches the metal bench where I have joined David. He nods, extends his right hand, and shakes mine.

"You are approved!" he crows.

I leap to my feet and grab the handle of my briefcase, preparing to lunge toward the sliding glass doors twenty feet away that lead to the now-deserted terminal and out a second set of glass doors that open out into the moist, inky August night. I can almost smell the ocean.

"Wait," the man calls out sharply. "You can't take the laptop."

What? Why?

"Cubans can't have computers."

David motions with his hand that he wants to talk privately. We step into a nearby corner.

"I will not leave my laptop with Cuban State Security," I mumble, anticipating what he would say. As we discuss what to do, a small-boned woman with a lined face and mussed hair approaches. I'd noticed her before watching my interrogation, chin on a broom handle, straining to hear my conversation with the security agents.

Head lowered, she glides toward us and, making sweeping motions with the broom, whispers, "Give it to him," and points at David.

"Foreigners can have computers."

I hand David my laptop and grab his hand.

"It's his," I say and smile at the security man as we walk past him and stroll like honeymooners out the sliding glass doors into the steamy moonlit Havana night. Home again.

*   *   *

A few days later, at a pizza restaurant some blocks from our hotel in the once posh, now shabby El Vedado neighborhood, I relate my airport interrogation to our friend Roberto, a balding middle-aged man with a high-level position at a government-run cultural institute. His wife oversees a government education department. Roberto looks uneasy as I explain that my travel license from the U.S. allows university professors, regardless of nationality, to travel to Cuba to do research.

Our faces were drenched in sweat; we spent a lazy hour talking to him inside the smoky restaurant. In pre-revolutionary times, El Vedado bustled with commerce, banks, embassies, and elegant Colonial mansions. When we stroll the torn-up sidewalks, strangers point up and caution us to watch for falling chunks from crumbling balconies. We dodge sidewalk potholes the size of bowling balls during walks on these streets to the Havana Libre hotel, the site of a casino owned by the U.S. mafia in the 1950s but now nicely remodeled for tourists and business executives, and to the well-known Copelia for scoops of vanilla ice-cream. We learn that some local vendors accept Cuban pesos—the nearly worthless currency for locals—while merchants that cater to tourists deal only in Cuban Convertible Pesos, each worth about 85 cents on the U.S. dollar.

As I retell the drama of the airport logjam, Roberto plucks a handkerchief from his breast pocket and wipes his shiny forehead. He crosses and uncrosses his legs. He clears his throat and leans toward me across the Formica top table.

"You needed a formal letter of invitation from a Cuban government organization," he says.

"Oh." The thought never crossed my mind.

"How come they let me in?"

"Because you are Cubana, with family here," he guffaws. The paperwork I brought with me was not worth the trouble.

* * *

I have worn a variety of identity labels throughout life, much as a hiker carries essential provisions in a backpack. I was "the Spanish girl" in third grade because I spoke Spanish, highlighting my status as a stranger in a foreign land. What they meant was that I was the girl from Cuba. I dutifully checked "Hispanic" or "Latino" in college on admitting and financial aid forms. In the U.S., I'm perceived as an exile, a Cuban American, or an immigrant because of my Latino name despite my blondish-brown hair and Robin's egg-blue eyes like my mother's. Before I pledged allegiance to America, my green card listed me as a resident alien.

When in Cuba, I am Cubana or Cubana-Americana. Other times, depending on the level of conflict between my two countries, I am viewed as a *gusana*, worm, a label given to anyone who fled Cuba after the revolution, or with suspicion as the Yankee enemy. I've worn these labels when I travel—hippie patches stitched to the back pocket of my jeans. Each classification serves a purpose as I navigate various stages of life and roles I've assumed: *niña*, child, student, English major, reporter, wife, *madre*, champion of diversity in newsrooms, and professor. I resent each one; they capture a narrow sliver of who I am and am yet to become. Sometimes they open the door to Cuba; other times, it's slammed shut.

My most authentic self is *guajira*, the Cuban term for poor, unsophisticated country folks like my parents who were born and bred in Guira de Melena, a farming village of cane stalks tall as giants with unpaved roads lined with thatch roof houses where chickens and roosters scratch the backyard dirt for dried rice and corn. My child self remains in Guira, an hour's drive east of Havana. People say the soil there is so red, mineral-rich, and pungent after a rainstorm that it leaves permanent stains on anything it touches. Once, during a visit to the coastal city of Cienfuegos, I mentioned where I was born to a tour guide.

"Oh," she grinned.

"Only dirt from Guira can remove the stains left by the red dirt from Guira." I laughed because I knew first-hand what she meant. When I was three, a jealous neighbor girl who was always allowed to go naked pushed me into a mud puddle after a summer rainstorm. The mud ruined my shoes, socks, and white linen dress. No matter how hard my mother scrubbed the clothes with lye soap in a backyard batea, the stubborn stains remained.

"I'm never letting you out to play with that nasty girl again," she admonished as she hunched over the washing pan. The canister of dirt from Guira I keep at home proves my original ground.

Dad, one of seven children of tenant farmers, left school in fourth grade to help his father and grandfather raise cattle and till the soil on a rented farm on the outskirts of Guira. Although they never owned the land—they called the farm *la Gloria*—God's reward after a hardscrabble life on the Canary Islands. In Guira, the family worked hard and saved their pennies to buy the twenty acres from the owners—wealthy Polish brothers from Havana. When Cuba's banks crashed in the 1920s, it wiped out their savings.

Presbyterian missionaries from America taught Dad to read and write. Mom was one step above Dad on the social ladder. While his family was dirt poor, hers had middle-class aspirations because her father, Simon Herrera, was the town's police officer who kept the peace and arbitrated petty disputes among his Black and white guajiro neighbors. Although respected and, to some extent, loved by the townspeople, he was stubborn and authoritarian and exhibited an explosive temper when faced with injustice. Family lore says Abuelo once came upon his superior officer whipping a Black man for stealing bananas. My grandfather ordered his sergeant to stop lashing the poor thief. The sergeant became enraged, drew his gun, and threatened to shoot Abuelo. Fate intervened. My grandmother Matilde happened to be passing by and witnessed the alarming episode.

She ran up to the officer, kneeled before him, wrapped her arms around his shiny boots, and begged him not to kill her husband because he would leave behind a widow and five children.

That demonstration of courage was uncharacteristic of Matilde, a submissive, uncomplaining woman who never smiled as she fulfilled the roles of wife, mother, cook, laundress, and housekeeper. She awoke before dawn, brewed a strong pot of café cubano on the carbon stove, and swept and washed all the house floors and the front porch before her husband and children arose to demand breakfast. Somehow she found time daily to brush and braid her four daughter's waist-length hair.

My patriarchal grandfather quashed my mother's desire to study at the University of Havana. Instead, she and her three sisters remained at home until they married—often to men selected by their father—and learned to sew and embroider—the only skills appropriate for *señoritas*, young ladies. But Mom inherited her father's tenacity and keen sense of Cuba's shifting politics that augured revolt. She believed her father's prognostication, spoken loudly and often to family, friends, and neighbors: "Cuba will someday be the first Communist country in this hemisphere." Mom was determined to leave before that happened.

After she married Dad, she scanned her bleak horizon—a rented wood frame, leaky, cockroach-infected *bahareque*, Dad's dollar-a-day salary hauling sugarcane and pineapples to far corners of the island for a rich hacendado, their mushrooming debt to the grocer, and her embarrassment each time her older sister brought over food and gave her money for clothes and shoes for her young daughters.

Nos vamos de este pais de mierda, she announced one day to Dad, covered in dirt and sweat from a three-day work trip to Pinar del Rio.

"We're leaving this shithole."

Shocked by Olga's strong language and the lightning flashes in her blue eyes, Dad stared at the floor and took a slow sip of water from the glass she handed him.

"We're not going anywhere," he said, slammed the water glass on the table, and marched out to the front porch.

Aquí me muero, "I will die here."

"That's what you think," Mom called after him and sat down at the kitchen table to write to Carmen, her widowed aunt who lived in Tampa, asking for help to leave. Eighteen months later, my parents appeared on the wood steps of her West Tampa rooming house with two battered suitcases, me and my two-year-old sister in tow.

I often explain to friends and acquaintances that my family left to escape poverty, not politics. I say this to distinguish my poor backwater family from the wealthy landowners, politicians, professionals, and middle-class exiles who lost land, homes, or businesses when they fled in the early '60s. I'm proud of my guajira origins and outsized social conscience, which sparked my desire to join the student brigades headed to Cuba after the revolution to cut cane for *la causa,* the cause. Instead, I attended the local college and studied Milton and Shakespeare. But my rash, left-leaning inclinations led to ex-communication by my parents, who did not allow me to visit them for a few years, even at Christmas. After they welcomed me back, I remained faithful to the revolution's idealism to protect the poor and fight for justice, equality, and land reform. Later, after I became a journalist and Castro and the revolution began to age, I became aware of the distance between my lofty beliefs and why my country, under constant aggression from its Capitalist neighbor, had turned Communist.

When I left Cuba with my family two years before the *revolucionarios* came to power, we lost nothing of material value—just our family of origin and Spanish-speaking culture—a far more significant loss, in my mind.

Later, we became exiles when my naïve, clueless parents returned to Cuba for a family visit during the Christmas holidays in 1958 and landed in the midst of la *robolución,* as my clever mom calls the cataclysmic event. The word is a pun on *robar,* to steal.

On that New Year's Eve, shortly before midnight, as we were about to go to sleep in my aunt and uncle's house in suburban Guanabacoa, the wealthy and powerful Cuban elite waited across the bay in a gangster-owned oceanfront hotel to celebrate *año nuevo* with the soon-to-arrive Fulgencio Batista, the corrupt and broadly disliked Cuban President. He never showed up. Instead, he stole away with his family, political cronies, and suitcases stuffed with pesos from the national treasury on a military plane to the Dominican Republic. We were awakened by an explosion that rocked our neighborhood sometime after midnight. The powerful blast kicked my pregnant mother off the bed. At the time, we had no clue what caused the explosion. Decades later, as I scoured old newspapers in a Cuban library, I learned the cause of the blast. Before they fled, Batista soldiers dynamited the nearby armory stocked with guns and ammunition to prevent the arms from falling into the hands of the triumphant *milicianos*.

The following day, radio stations crackled with news of Batista's stealthy midnight flight, and newspaper headlines screamed the approaching arrival in Havana of a brash young lawyer turned-revolutionary named Fidel Castro and his fighting men. Cheering rambunctious crowds piled into the city and suburban streets shouting revolutionary slogans. *Patria o Muerte, Venceremos*—country or death, we shall prevail—the people pronounced proudly as they poured into Old Havana to glimpse the handsome *comandante* who had fought bravely in the Sierra and prevailed to save them from *pobreza* and *corrupcion*.

My family joined the exuberant marchers on the jammed streets for several hours before my worried parents insisted my uncle drive us back to Guira. Mom voiced a suspicion that the so-called people's revolution would turn dark purple, violent, and Communist; Dad wanted to make sure his widowed mother and siblings were safe. After we returned to Guira, we shuttered the windows and doors and huddled in the living room with our relatives, glued to the stand-up radio in the corner of the living room. Radio Reloj broadcast continuous reports out of Havana—angry mobs storming casinos, smashing gambling machines and parking meters, a national work strike, house searches, looting of the fancy downtown El Encanto department store and other Batista-friendly shops and businesses. One afternoon, a young cousin strolled into our house to proudly display a jar of buttons he'd pilfered from a nearby ransacked garment factory. The factory's owner was a local woman, a Batista supporter, and had been close friends with my family.

"La puta deserved it," the boy crowed. The English for *puta* is whore.

Fearing a mass exodus of Batista cronies with jewel-stuffed pockets and jackets lined with stolen *billetes*, the victors shut down the airport. When flights resumed a month later, we boarded the first Pan American flight back to Florida. We bid farewell to my grandmother and other relatives at the airport, our cheeks stained by tears, our open hands separated by an impenetrable wall of plexiglass. The pain of separation that day hurt more than my bruised finger that got caught in the seam of the glass front door of the U.S. Embassy.

Dad didn't want to leave; take a chance on the promise of the revolution. My willful, practical Mom disagreed. "*Nos vamos*," she insisted. "We are leaving no matter what." Had we stayed, what would have happened to us, I wonder? Indeed a radically different life.

During the '60s and '70s, when we could not return because of the fractured politics between my homeland and adopted country, my grandmothers Matilde and Florinda died. We learned of their death by telegram. The only other means of communication with extended family was by letter, post-dated by one or more months. Phone calls were expensive, and the unreliable ATT underwire cables between Florida and the island crackled and wheezed and sometimes died during short conversations. We pored over their handwritten missives at the kitchen table like Bible scripture. The tear-stained volumes—ten pages or longer written in blue ballpoint on both sides of the thin-lined sheets in stiff, cramped cursive—informed us of births, deaths, and weddings. The *por avion* envelopes were stuffed with photos of birthdays, weddings, and newborns. Some included crudely made brown paper greeting cards for

Mother's Day or Navidad. Mom kept them in a pink and white Formica cabinet drawer lined our bathroom wall next to the eat-in galley kitchen. As a child, I spent hours reviewing family photos, an exercise for my faltering memory.

Our enforced exile ended in the late '70s when one-term President Jimmy Carter and Fidel Castro eased travel restrictions for Cuban Americans, and air caravans of exiles poured out of Miami airport into the island. The former "traitors" were now welcome. They carried wads of U.S. dollars, bars of chocolate, baby aspirin, and Japanese-made consumer goods in worm-shaped duffle bags wrapped in plastic they called *gusanos*. We left as *gusanos; now* we return *with* gusanos, joked the returnees. When my parents and I visited for the first-time post '59 on one of the family reunification flights, we, too, carried overstuffed duffels. Mom wore five pairs of underpants beneath her wide skirt, and Dad stuffed bags of Bustelo coffee in his jacket pockets.

* *

Guira de Melena, Cuba, May 1979

I have become aware during this trip—the first in over twenty years—of the linguistic hierarchy in my head—English first, Spanish second. Although my parents are not as Americanized as I am, the prolonged absence has changed them too. With their U.S. clothes and smattering of English, I experience a sense that we are simultaneously living in the past and present. Dad wears a tan-colored tweed sports jacket from J.C. Penney daily, even to the call-and-response *canturia* organized one evening by two of his brothers to welcome us home. In his youth, my father was a well-regarded guajiro poet and bard. He penned copious ten-line décimas, which he sang to the strum of his guitar at country fairs, backyard pig roasts, and once on the radio in Havana. In Florida, he still scrawls poems in a small black notebook tucked in his breast pocket next to a pen and a shiny black plastic comb.

Tonight he hangs back even though he is the star of the show.

A poet friend asks him to play the guitar and extemporize as he had in his youth when he was known as *el sinsonte*, the songbird of Guira. Dad grins.

"I parked my guitar in a corner the day I left Cuba," he says, a silly smile slapped on his face.

After more cajoling, Dad croons several of his pre-exile décimas in honor of Florinda, his deceased mother, another about an old cow without a tail his father sold to a gullible *guajiro*, and a politically incorrect one he wrote in Tampa promising to go naked for a year when Castro dies or leaves. This one brings nervous titters from the crowd.

I notice that Dad says "shurrr" and "jes" a lot instead of "sí" or "cómo no," of course. With her modern perm and red-manicured nails, Mom looked radiant and youthful alongside her sad-eyed fatigued-looking sisters. She deals bars of Dove soap and plastic packets of oregano to her female relatives as deftly as a poker player. My father's three brothers and other male relatives and friends receive yellow Bic shavers—they are amazed and amused by these marvelous technological wonders—and toothbrushes wrapped in cellophane.

I answer my relatives' questions about life in America. In one conversation, they want to know about the existence of racism.

An aunt's husband inquires if a white person can be jailed in the U.S. for helping or touching a black person. He says he read this in the Cuban press. This man is a war veteran in Angola, a staunch Communist. We converse in his living room, between us a glass-top coffee table with pictures of revolutionary heroes Che Guevara and Camilo Cienfuegos.

I explain that racial discrimination still exists in the U.S. but that blacks and whites have equal rights under the law.

"We no longer have separate water fountains or bathrooms for blacks and whites," I explain. "Blacks attend college alongside whites."

He isn't convinced.

I go on long strolls with my chattering teenage cousins through the sugar cane fields and grand pre-revolutionary haciendas just outside of town. They mention casually that the land we walk on was farmed for decades by Dad's family, the Arochas. They tell me a story I've never heard. Shortly before the revolution, when La Gloria farm's wealthy absentee owners decided to leave the country, they gifted the farm and the manor house to Dad's father and uncle. It was a verbal commitment, nothing put down on paper, and after land reform, all but one of Dad's siblings agreed to leave the farm in exchange for a new concrete block house in the center of town. All but Juana, Dad's 80-year-old sister. She still clings to her tumbledown, thatched roof *bohio* that sits on a patch of red dirt at the edge of the farm.

When I visit, she waits for me on a rocker on the front porch. She wears a worn, faded cotton shift.

"I plan to stay 'til I die," she hisses and points to the flimsy floorboards of her porch beneath her bare feet. Her faded brown eyes grow expansive and dreamy as if she were calling up a long-ago mirage of a pretty teenage girl walking barefoot behind her older brother to a country *canturia*.

"Your Dad was a hell of a poet," she chortles. "The best." I nod in agreement.

Later, my cousins and I wander around the boarded-up manor house, previously a summer home for the Havana owners of the farm, known only as *los polacos*, the poles. No one knows or remembers their real names.

An empty backyard pool behind the house is filled with rotting leaves, dead branches, and debris. They say the local government converted the now-abandoned house into a restaurant a while ago. No one came, and the government closed it.

My pre-teen cousins possess an intricate knowledge of modern American culture, primarily through videos and music CDs smuggled into Cuba by visiting U.S. relatives. They mention Hollywood movies they have somehow seen or heard about—Star Wars, The Terminator, and Friday the 13th. They recite American movie plots by heart and speak in familiar terms of Arnold Schwarzenegger, Luke Skywalker, and Freddy Krueger, just as my parents still recall the Latin American and Spanish movie stars from their youthful era—Cantinflas, Maria Felix, Sarita Montiel. We watched these mega stars perform each Sunday afternoon in comedies, romantic dramas, and adventure films on the big screen of a musty ornate theater in Ybor City, settled by Cuban cigar workers in the 19th century and considered the heart and soul of Tampa's immigrant community.

My cousins beg me to return and bring them *pitusas*, blue jeans, and music cassettes of the Grateful Dead and The Rolling Stones. One night a family friend hooks up a contraband cassette player to a dangling electric wire behind his house, and we dance in the middle of the red dirt street to Y.M.C.A. and Girl From Ipanema until one in the morning.

I rediscover the taste of raw sugar cane on my tongue. The earthy smell of *fruta bomba, mango, cherimoya*. The scent of jasmine and my grandmother's marigolds and ancient roses. I listen in awe to the melodious crowing of cocks at sunrise and sometimes as the sun sets. Everything I see, taste, and hear is magical, fresh, and newborn, imbued by a startling radiance like steam rising from a sunlit meadow after a brief summer storm. I rediscover the lush tropical landscape of childhood, still ripe with promise. I've met dozens of cousins I never knew. Even my grandparents' home and the rickety house we lived in when I was born appear precious and exotic, never mind the holes in their roofs, the lack of indoor plumbing, and the unpaved, muddy street in front that floods whenever it rains. Never mind the whispered warnings from our loved ones not to talk politics or mention *el nombre de ese hombre*, that man's name, even indoors.

* *

Cuba is an ambivalent lover; she wants me, she wants me not. In a tune from the pre-50s era, one lover says to the other: "Whenever I ask you when, how, where you always respond, perhaps, perhaps, perhaps." The song, performed by Nat King Cole in English in the 50s, reminds me of my mother begging my reluctant father for us to leave their country. Although instead of perhaps, he always said no. Like a long-abused partner, I cling to my homeland's sometimes phony kisses and counterfeit hugs. It's been an on-again, off-again life-long affair even after decades of *separación*, a word that captures the heartbreak of separation for most Cuban families.

Another famous Cuban son, *Regreso del Amor*, The Return of Love, provides a reason for thwarted love.

It goes:

I gave you my soul

you gave me yours

We were happy together

Until enemies separated us

But our love forever grows.

Divergent political ideologies ended the once-close relationship between my two countries. A more appropriate title for that melancholy tune: Cuba and the U.S., enemies, a love story.

* *

Tampa, Florida, 1977

I sit at my desk in the newsroom of *The Tampa Times*, taking bites from a homemade tuna sandwich, when the phone rings.

"Hola, Cuba on the line," says a scratchy female voice, followed by several clicks and a long silence."

"Hola, hola," says the thin voice that fades in and out as if submerged under the ocean. "Are you there?"

"Who is this," I blurt out.

"It's the Cuban Department of State."

"Who?" I ask, in my now steady professional-sounding voice.

"The Cuban State Department. We're inviting you and other Cuban American journalists to Havana for an international gathering of students. Will you come?"

I accept and dash into my editor's glass-enclosed office to ask permission. Bruce, who has a reputation for hitting on pretty young reporters with big boobs, is less than enthusiastic about spending money for a story more relevant in Miami than on the West Coast of Florida.

"It's a good story," I argue, bat my eyes, and explain that I have not returned to my homeland since the revolution. I still have family there.

"Besides," I add, "a strong Tampa-Cuba connection dates to the start of the world-known cigar industry that began in the 1880s in Ybor City." He wasn't convinced but finally said yes.

A month later, I flew to Miami for the trip home with two other Cuban American journalists—Guillermo Martinez and Ileana Oroza—from *El Herald*, the Spanish section of *The Miami Herald*. We are scheduled to catch a commuter flight to Havana at 4 p.m.

Two hours before take-off, Havana calls.

"Lo siento," we're sorry, says the unnamed voice on the telephone.

"The trip is canceled." No explanation.

The aborted trip wasn't a total loss. Although Fidel stood me up, I met my future husband David, an editor at the paper. I landed a job in Miami six months later to cover the political intrigue brewing in Little Havana. When I told my editor Bruce I was leaving Tampa, he harrumphed, walked away, and never spoke to me again.

* *

As *The Miami Herald*'s first bilingual, U.S.-educated Cuban American journalist, I reported on the early contacts between a group of Cubans in exile—El Comité de los 75—and the Cuban government. This controversial group of Cuban American academics, journalists, artists, lawyers, ministers, bankers, and businessmen sought to negotiate the release of political prisoners and crack open the door for exiles to return for visits to the island. They traveled to Cuba several times to speak with Fidel. The dialogue produced a U.S.-government-sanctioned deal.

Miami's Spanish radio airwaves soon crackled 24-7 with diatribes calling the men and women *dialogueros*, traitors, and spies, accusing them of being *agentes*, agents of Fidel. Why else would a patriotic exile agree to sit and talk with *el enemigo barbudo*, the bearded enemy?

Soon after the dialogue started, bombs exploded outside travel agencies, businesses in Miami, New Jersey, and Puerto Rico, and even outside a bank in Little Havana. Several of the *dialogueros* were threatened; at least two were killed. As I reported on this, my parents in Tampa became worried.

Mom rang me at the office one day.

"Do you know what they are saying about you on the radio?" she gasped.

She'd just heard a top radio commentator in Miami vow to silence "that Cuban reporter from *The Miami Herald*." They repeated my name.

"He called you a Communist," Mom shrieked.

I reassured her I didn't listen to Cuban exile radio. The right-wing ideologues preferred verbal intimidation to action.

"I'm fine," I said. "You shouldn't worry either."

The rapprochement between the moderate exiles and the Cuban government resulted in the opening of half a dozen storefront travel agencies in Little Havana, Hialeah, and elsewhere. The roundtrip charter flights cost $500 or more and, at first, were peddled by a charismatic preacher with dubious credentials and fiery rhetoric. The motive behind Reverend Manuel Espinoza's sermons at his fundamentalist church inside a Hialeah warehouse was not about saving souls but about "family reunification." The true believers who attended services were primarily middle-aged Cuban women longing to see mothers, fathers, siblings, and children after long years of separation. They jumped up from their gray folding chairs, lifted their arms toward the blinding fluorescent lights in the ceiling, and chanted "viajes a Cuba" as the pseudominister preached about the love of family and ending the decades-long suffering of separation.

I interviewed the charming half-cocked minister many times. The interviews were more like rapid-fire informal monologues punctuated with colorful curse words directed at his enemies on the right who opposed any rapprochement with the island.

I asked about the closed-circuit cameras on his warehouse church's front and back doors, the seven-foot walls, half dozen bodyguards, and police dogs outside his home near the improvised temple.

"I've received many threats," he said, lowered his voice, leaned toward me, and stretched his arms across the metal desktop.

"Those *hijos de puta* want me dead," he hissed.

"They preach hate. I preach love."

Espinosa boasted that the exile trips were his brainchild. A few years earlier, he told me, he'd evaded the U.S. Coast Guard and landed a rented motorboat on the Cuban coast near Camaguey. Cuban patrols captured him before he placed one foot on dry land. After weeks of interrogation in a Cuban jail cell, he convinced his captors that he wasn't a spy for the gringos. Instead, he wanted to sell them a novel scheme to generate U.S. dollars for the failing Cuban economy and bypass the U.S. trade embargo. He proposed that Cuba allow Cuban Americans to return to visit their relatives, bringing them suitcases with consumer goods and, most importantly, thousands of greenbacks. The plan was risky, but the Cubans bought it.

A short time later, Espinoza was back in Miami, peddling *viajes* a Cuba. Soon another evangelical minister and half a dozen exiled entrepreneurs in Miami, New Jersey, and Puerto Rico began to sell the lucrative family trips to Cuba.

Hundreds, then thousands, of exiles began to return home on jammed charter flights that departed several days a week from Miami International Airport. The family reunification trips continue today, and some conservative Cubans still argue that they violate the U.S. trade embargo and serve to prop up the financially strapped repressive regime. Before the Trump administration imposed strict restrictions in 2020 on how much money Cuban Americans could send relatives on the island, family remittances contributed nine hundred million to one-and-a-half billion dollars annually to the Cuban economy, among the top three sources of foreign income.

* *

.My first return to the island was a 24-hour reporting trip organized by Espinoza, whom people called el *reverendo*, the reverend. Our mission was to pick up some just-released prisoners and fly them to Miami. Espinoza, two pilots, and I were the only ones on board the Miami-Havana-bound 737 charter flight late one afternoon in early 1979. I felt goosebumps as the plane touched down on the runway I'd left from in 57 and again in 59. A taxi drove us from the airport through dim, deserted streets to the Central Havana home of a just-released prisoner. At that time, Cuba had started to ration electricity, and the hulking unfamiliar city buildings rushing past us on the unlit streets looked like scenes from a grainy black-and-white silent movie. Later, I sat nervously on a lumpy sofa in the half shadows created by a naked lightbulb in the man's sparse living room—a circle of family and friends surrounded him. I heard sobbing from the back room. The conversation was strained with awkward silences and occasional whispers. I was afraid to ask many questions, assuming the government was listening.

As we waited for the dawn, a woman offered us coffee. I am still trying to remember where or if I slept that night. I boarded an early morning plane with thirty released prisoners and their family members. *El reverendo* said he was staying for "more talks."

When our plane touched down in Miami, everyone cheered and clapped. Most wept. I still tasted ocean salt on my tongue.

* *

Each trip home entails a slight shift in identity, a different outside image of "me" created by moving mirrors inside the kaleidoscope of U.S.-Cuba relations. The prism of politics and the lingering political, social, and historic Cold War forces beyond my puny control distorts my identity. The kaleidoscope shifts with each major or minor news event—an early morning CIA-engineered invasion by exiles at the Bay of Pigs—Cubans call it Playa Girón; a nuclear showdown between the U.S. and the Soviets over missiles on the island; a Cuban exile pilot shot out of the sky by the Cuban military quashing hopes of a rapprochement with the U.S.; the young boy Elian Gonzalez brought to the U.S. by his mother who died during the crossing and was returned by force to his father in Cuba; the arrest of a Cuban spy caught working in the Defense Intelligence Agency, the arrest of an alleged U.S. spy in Cuba. And many other diplomatic pivot points in the fraught relationship. Buddhists believe that the actions of humans, families, and countries produce karma—the notion that you reap what you sow. I think Cuba's karma is resistance—America's dominance.

The Mariel Boatlift of the 80s, when Cuba dumped 125,000 Cubans on an unsuspecting Washington, was a near-fatal blow to closer relations between the two countries. Although a few were ordinary prisoners and mental patients, Cuba called all who left *escoria*, garbage. Crafty exiles like Espinosa played both sides to advantage. After the boatlift, when U.S.-Cuba relations soured, and the oversaturated tourism business to

Cuba slowed, the previously cocky now chastened Espinoza went on the Miami airwaves to denounce, by name, the multitude of Castro spies living in their midst, most of them former friends and business acquaintances. Every week he added new names to the list. Espinoza died a few years later. His obit said from a heart attack.

Several years ago, under President Obama, the archenemies kissed and made up, renewed diplomatic ties, reopened their embassies, and began cooperating on bilateral tourism, cultural, and education exchange. The U.S. eased travel restrictions for average Americans to visit Cuba and allowed some U.S. businesses, including airlines and cruise ships, to enter the Cuban tourism market. Obama also eased the cap on how much money in remittances Cuban Americans could send to relatives. Cuba, in turn, began to grant business licenses to thousands of ordinary citizens who turned their homes into restaurants and Airbnb's, home bakeries, watch and bicycle repair shops, and allowed artisans to sell their crafts, jewelry, and clothing to foreign visitors.

A U.S. President visited the outlaw island for the first time in 60 years. Obama met with his counterpart, Raul Castro, and even enjoyed a baseball game alongside the Cuban President. Friendlier relations ended when Donald Trump assumed the presidency. He reversed most of Obama's more open policies on travel and remittances. Although Joe Biden softened some of Trump's sanctions against Cuba, another rapprochement appears unlikely for many reasons, including future United States elections, partisan politics, and the fact that both parties must pander to the conservative and wealthy Cuban American lobby for coveted votes. According to recent polls, Americans generally support closer ties with Cuba, as do younger generations of Cubans. But the aging and dwindling number of anti-Castro die-hards still believe the U.S. has sold out to the Communists in Havana. Many Cuban American political leaders share their outdated ideology. Finally, a U.S. president cannot unilaterally lift the decades-old economy-crippling U.S. embargo against Cuba—Cuba calls it a blockade. Only an act of Congress can remove it.

In Havana, a new generation of less ideologically inclined Cuban leaders is being led by Diaz Canal, a younger president not connected to the Castro family. In the post-COVID environment, the Cuban economy remains dangerously unstable. The country's shift to a unified currency, combined with severe shortages of food, consumer goods, and medicine, were significant factors in mass protests that erupted during the summer of 2021, prompting a brutal government crackdown. Last year, more than a hundred thousand Cubans—a number greater than those that fled during the Mariel boatlift—have left on boats bound for Florida or traveled dangerous routes on foot through South and Central America to the U.S.-Mexico border.

What will the future bring?

After Cubans voted for a new constitution in 2019, politicians insisted they were not giving up on but perfecting their hard-won revolution.

As a tour guide once said to a group of visiting U.S. teachers and students: "We want Socialism with *pachanga*."

Pachanga means party.

My countrymen and women remain hopeful that their exuberant Afro-Cuban spirit is compatible with their chosen political form of left-leaning government.

* *

Havana, May 1979

Mom, Dad, I plop down on the double beds of our room at the worn but still elegant Havana Libre hotel—where Fidel and his closest advisors, including Ché Guevara, camped out for several months to create a new government. We fly back to Florida in the morning.

Beneath the warm glow of the lamp on the nightstand, we reflect on the roller-coaster week in Guira—the scarcity of food, the state of our relatives' health, the run-down condition of my grandparent's house, the empty shelves of the once well-stocked stores along our town's dusty main road—the whispers behind closed doors.

"Is it like you remembered?" I ask.

"Qué va," Dad shakes his head; no way.

"I'm never returning."

Mom chuckles.

"We're leaving with just the clothes on our backs—like the first time," she says, recalling how we've given away all our belongings from the duffels to our relatives.

She grows quiet, sighs, and lowers her voice. Walls have ears, we've heard.

"The Cuba I knew is gone."

I don't argue or ask her why.

Gone too is my remembered country, a four-year-old child who long ago sat on her grandfather's lap watching smoke rings rise and disappear near the ceiling as she sips the last *buchito de café* from his miniature teacup. The brief recollected vision vanishes like the clouds of cigar smoke, but my compulsive neurotic heart is not ready to let her go. I am already planning the next trip in my head.

CHAPTER 2

BILONGO

Tampa, Florida, 1961

When I was nine, my mother feared demons possessed me. She had good reason to worry and, out of desperation, took me to see a Cuban santero for a *despojo* to rid me of the evil spirits she was convinced had seized me.

My mental state then was a vast closet of bizarre and twisted fears, real and imagined. My body suffered mysterious symptoms and ailments: rivulets of sweat pouring from my palms, diffuse and powerful stomach aches, shooting pains down my legs, fainting, sleepwalking, and peeing in bed.

At night I'd lie in my twin bed, with a sheet bound tight around my neck, scanning the room for fanged monsters, silvery ghosts, and other menacing *demonios* that lurked behind the red-and-white paisley curtains outside the Sears replacement window above my head, under the mattress and in the corner crevices of the cramped bedroom I shared with my sleeping sister. I fought to stay awake as ferociously as if I were one of Fidel's guerrilla fighters looking for dreaded Batista soldiers. Most terrifying was the fear that I would die if I fell asleep.

When I could no longer count on willpower to stay awake, I'd call out for my dad, who was asleep in the back room of our *cañon* shotgun house. They are called shotgun houses because each was the same: a front door, a back door, and a series of skinny rooms in between; fire a gun or cannon through the front door, and the bullet or cannonball exited out the back. Dad would materialize beside me, cradle my small hand in his broad, rough one, and croon a *punto guajiro*, a country ballad about his homeland Cuba. One poem was about his only return trip to Guira de Melena—*mi cuna*, my cradle, he called it—after twenty years as an immigrant in Florida.

Lulled by this and other melodic verses, I began to nod and fell asleep after midnight.

The peculiar fear of dying in slumber lasted months, vanished one day as enigmatically as it had arrived, but morphed into panics and heart-pounding nightmares that sent me dashing down the linoleum tiled hallway, dodging Mom's ceramic four-foot statues of peasant girls carrying baskets of green plastic grapes on the way to my parent's bedroom.

"I'm scared," I whimpered outside their closed door.

"Silly, *no seas miedosa*, go back to bed," Mom barked, twirled her curler-covered head toward the wall and ignored me. Dad was sympathetic. As a young husband on the island and later in exile, his soul sometimes flew from his body to who knows where. He refused to eat, bathe or go to work for days or weeks. Reclining in bed in this senseless, cata-tonic state, his eyes half closed, he lacked the strength or will to drag himself to the kitchen table or answer my mother's harangues about the rent payment coming due and the depleted kitchen cupboards—"Your daughters need to eat," she reminded him. Eventually, he would rise from the bed, shower, dress, slog out the door, a box of plumber's tools under an arm, and climb behind the wheel of his prized second-hand *troque*. A Ford truck paid for with years of savings from his plumber's salary. The beloved trustworthy vehicle kept him going, always waiting for him in the two-car garage. His depression—that's what it was, I learned much later— was treated once at the Ybor City immigrant clinic we belonged to. The Spanish-speaking doctor—Mom called them *mediq-uitos*, little doctors, to distinguish them from the real doctors (usually White) with downtown skyscraper offices—prescribed mega doses of vitamin B shots twice a week for a month. They worked until another dark spell descended as sure as the next chime of the grandfather clock we had purchased on layaway in Ybor City.

Dad and I devised a secret game to circumvent my mother's cold refusal to let me sleep in their bed. I waited outside their door until I was sure she'd fallen back to sleep, stepped lightly on the beige shag rug, and slinked quietly as an alley cat after a *ratón* to Dad's side of the bed. I would burrow under the covers and eventually fall asleep. Before dawn, I'd scurry back to my bed so Mom wouldn't catch on.

I was terrified not just of the phantasmagorical but of perceived material dangers: large barking dogs, the aggressive rooster in our backyard who chased after me when I came home from school, my slightly off piano teacher, and our nosey across-the-street neighbor. Nick was a war veteran who'd brought back a Korean wife and would peer from behind the heavy floral drapes of his living room picture window whenever I walked past on my way to school. His creepy behavior lasted throughout my teenage years when he turned his spying eyes on the boys who visited us when our parents were at work. Somehow Mom always knew about the illicit visits of boys to our house; I figured Nick was the tattletale.

After the Cuban Missile Crisis in 1964 ended a hair's breadth away from nuclear Armageddon, I began to panic that the dreaded *bomba* was about to incinerate our Italian-Black-Cuban neighborhood, our tin-roof, hot-as-blazes bungalow, all of us inside, even the cockroaches underneath in the crawl space and the chickens in the yard. This fear lasted longer than a year.

Family trips to down-at-the-heels Ybor City—in its heyday, the world capital of Cuban cigars and in the '60s and '70s still the heart and soul of Cuban and Italian expatriates who once hand-made them—also caused dread.

Our frequent bus visits to the immigrant enclave included checkups at the Bien Público Clinic, once-a-year family portraits, and cups of steaming café con leche at sidewalk store windows, ended with a stop at the Woolworth's department store, where I browsed the Trixie Belden and Nancy Drew shelves while Mom shopped. If I lost sight of her for more than a few seconds, my imagination concocted alarming scenarios of the store closing with poor me, *pobrecita*, trapped inside all night—an adventure a less fearful child would have relished.

Faster than a startled *conejo* in a summer garden, off I bounded to find my mother, whom I discovered strolling some aisle in single-minded pursuit of a push-up bra or Cover Girl face powder.

"*Que te pasa?* What's wrong?" she asked in alarm as she peered at my beet-red face and dilating pupils.

"*Nada.* Nothing," I muttered. "I got scared."

"Stay close," she admonished and resumed hunting through the underwear shelves while my hand stayed glued to her skirt.

I figured out a clever way at school to disguise my out-of-the-blue panics and infrequent fainting spells. One incident was in first grade as I stared at a cold plate of peas in the school cafeteria.

"Eat your peas, children," Mrs. Moore, the teacher, barked from the head of the lunchroom table where I sat with my classmates. I squirmed and stared at the concrete floor. I hated the metallic taste of peas; the word sounded to my Spanish-attuned ears like "piss."

As I forced myself to swallow a forkful, an awful thought seized me: what if I AM already dead but don't know it, and EVERYONE here is dead too? I'd recently watched with my sister a horror film, "Night of the Living Dead," where ordinary people turn into zombies and feed on the flesh of the living. Foreboding dread sent me racing to Mrs. Moore.

"I am not feeling well," I muttered, staring at my Oxford shoes. She promptly sent me to a closet-sized cubicle next to the primary school office, where the nurse had me lay down on a green cot and placed alcohol-soaked gauze pads over my mouth and nose to bring me back to life.

She was kind and let me remain until the school bell rang. Afterward, the tiny infirmary became a frequent hideout.

In seventh grade, a disturbing film we were forced to watch about the dangers of venereal disease sent me loping outside the cafeteria to avoid passing out.

As we watched, I began to feel queasy; my heart thumped, and my breath grew shallow. What I'd eaten for lunch—a hotdog and fries—began to lurch toward my esophagus, and invisible ants seemed to be racing up and down my legs. My feet were numb.

Calmate, keep calm, I tried saying to myself. These feelings will disappear if you lay your head on the lunchroom table and cover it with your arms. After a while, I felt calmer, and I lifted my head to resume watching. I was fine until images of foot-long cranberry-colored rashes, warts, and oozing sores on genitalia flickered across the screen.

"This is what happens when teens have sex," the narrator boomed.

My head hit the table with a loud twang.

You are going to faint; you are fainting; get up, get out before you faaaa..., a voice in my head urged.

"Don't feel well," I croaked out loud and ran to the heavy gray metal double doors, dashed toward the uncovered walkway where I melted like a heap of wax on the hot concrete.

I waited several minutes to catch my breath and steady my wobbly legs, then bolted to the nurse's office, where I crumpled into the by-now familiar gray plastic chair by the door.

"What is it now?" inquired the nurse, her steady voice revealing a touch of exasperation because I'd been there earlier that week and the week before.

"I was going to faint," I said, exhaling loudly but omitting the reasons for my distress. I couldn't risk my classmates discovering that the sex-ed film had made me ill. This would undoubtedly seal my reputation as the alien girl from Cuba.

More distressing than the panic attacks and oversized fears was my uncontrollable sweating. I write this sentence, and my palms become moist, an instinctive physical reaction to the memory of shame this caused me.

Each morning, whenever I stepped out the back door into the scraggly yard, past our chickens and *the* dreaded rooster scratching for dried corn in the grainy gray dirt, walked through the wrought-iron driveway gate to the street, paused to wave at Nick peering from behind his heavy drapes, and headed west on St. John, my street, for the ten-block walk to the junior high, my hands turned to spigots.

When I neared the chain-link fence around the school's kickball fields, the drops of sweat had become a waterfall as potent as El Nicho back home. *Chorros* of perspiration cascaded down my palms and left round damp spots the size of quarters on my cotton skirt. The moisture created ugly, washed-out half-moon stains on the blue, green, yellow, black, and red folders—one for each school subject— that I clutched in my hands and pressed against my chest like a disintegrating paper breastplate. The ink leached onto my fingers and palms. Red was the cruelest color. When I arrived at first-period homeroom, my palms were the color of pomegranates. They were proof—I was confident, beyond a shadow of a doubt—that I was strange, *más loca que Juana*, my parents' expression from the old country about a crazy woman, Juana, who was so disturbed her family had her committed to Mazorra, the island's mental hospital.

I sat stiffly at my desk, concealed the dye-streaked hands in the folds of my pleated skirt, and prayed the teacher would not ask us to write in a notebook or send me to the chalkboard to solve a math problem. This would require me to reveal the shameful foreign objects hiding in my lap. If the teacher were to ask why my palms were bright red like the stripes in the American flag, what would I say? The red clay in the town where I was born does not wash out.

With my by-then unaccented English, blonde-brown hair, light skin, and blue eyes inherited from my grandfather and mother —traits common among northern Spaniards—people assume I come from Ohio or Indiana. If I wanted to, I could pass for Anglo-American. But I have become touchy about my background and ethnicity.

Later in life, as I walked into the news editor's office for a job interview, the man blurted: "You don't look Cuban!"

Instead of snapping back, I calmly filled in the apparent gaps in his understanding of Cuban racial history. When I told my father about the incident, he furrowed his brow.

"*Comemierda!*" he proclaimed, using a favorite expression among my compatriots for assholes, which means shit eater. I appreciated his saying what I had only thought.

Despite my easy-to-fit-in Anglo looks, I knew I *was* different, unlike the white and second and third-generation Italian children I attended school with who had learned English when they wore diapers. My schoolmates shopped for dresses at Maas Brothers, a fancy department store downtown, attended Girl Scouts meetings after school, and sold cookies on weekends at the Winn Dixie. They went on organized field trips with their scout leader to exotic places like Six Gun Territory and Weeki Wachee Springs, where passengers onboard glass-bottom boats gawked at voluptuous women dressed as mermaids who swam gracefully alongside the fish. The Anglo tradition of children selling cookies to pay for fun trips seemed a tad unusual, but I wanted to be a Girl Scout so I could join them. When I mentioned this to my financially stretched parents, they demurred. Later, they pointed out the obvious: we could not afford the required uniform—the olive-green skirt, white blouse buttoned at the front, and chest sash I coveted so much. I was sad but understood their everyday struggle to earn money for basics. So I waited until fifth grade, became a safety patrol, and wore a yellow chest sash with a shiny badge.

The nagging struggle for money drove my parents to search for ways to augment their working-class salaries. They came up with a brilliant idea—they would make tamales at home and sell them to friends and neighbors. Every Friday night and half day on Saturday for a few years, in a lean-to behind our kitchen, my parents worked to produce *casuelas* brimming with steaming, flavorful tamales. They shucked the fresh corn, ground the kernels into mush, flavored it with sofrito and chunks of fried pork, and wrapped the mixture in moistened corn husks tied with sturdy brown string. They boiled the bundles on a converted kerosene heater in a metal lard can. When the tamales were done, Dad placed the still-steaming kettles in the back of his turquoise and blue station wagon and drove slowly down the shady red brick streets of West Tampa, selling them for $1.25 each. The Cuban families who lived along our road and in our barrio were familiar with a popular song about a woman named Olga, like my mom, who sold tamales. Decades later, my parents' former clients from our Tampa neighborhood smack their lips when they recall *los tamalitos que vende Olga.*

The money they earned—$100 or more each weekend and unreported to Tío Sam—helped buy shoes, clothes, and school supplies and even paid for piano lessons. Eventually, a neighbor reported us to the health department, and we had to shut down the illegal business. Mom suspected that the *chismosa* who turned them in was a neighbor who also made and sold tamales on the side.

A cultural and language chasm separated me from my schoolmates throughout my school years. Mom made our clothes on a Singer sewing machine at the kitchen table after we cleared the dinner dishes. She tied green and red ribbons in my Shirley Temple curls before I left for school, just like other mothers had done in Cuba. Instead of milk and Cheerios to help "Get Yourself Go," my *desayuno* was a tall glass of sweetened *café con leche* and a slice of white bread slathered in butter.

My friends' parents spoke perfect English, mine only Spanish. However, Dad attended night school where he struggled, not with backed-up toilets and leaky faucets, but with the complexities of *in glii ssh*, which was way too hard for an unschooled *guajiro* who didn't learn to read and write until age 12. He beamed the day he passed his master plumber's test in English with an almost perfect score. We celebrated with chocolate-dipped vanilla ice cream cones from the Dairy Cream around the corner.

After my sister and I began taking piano lessons at the Debussy School of Music, my tense, prickly, and loony teacher reflected my fear that I was going mad.

Miss Marie, who was in her 50s and unmarried, ran the school with her brother, Mister Anthony, a soft-spoken taciturn bachelor in his 50s. Funny, we never knew their last names.

"Miss Marie was a famous concert pianist in the old country," Mister Anthony crowed the day my parents signed my sister and me up for the $5-a-week lessons. "She once performed in a concert hall in New York." Learning that helped seal the deal.

Over the coming months, Miss Marie taught me to play scales and simple tunes like *Clair de Lune* and the *Blue Danube Waltz*.

"Again, again, again," she admonished with a scowl, rapping my knuckles with a ruler whenever I hit a wrong note—which occurred often. The teacher had a strange way of peering at me with saucer-like eyes from behind raccoon-shaped glasses that made me squirm. While my sister had cried and begged her way out of continuing the lessons, I decided to stick with it, not to displease my mother, who, as a young woman, always wanted to learn to play piano, or perhaps it came from my innate stubbornness.

After my parents dropped me off one day at the ranch house home and studio, Mister Anthony, not Miss Marie, stood beside the piano bench, tapping his slender fingers against the top of the upright.

"My sister has gone away to get better," he said gravely. "I will be your teacher now."

The elderly bachelor was kind, easygoing, and rarely corrected me, unlike Miss Marie and the new arrangement suited me fine.

A few months later, Miss Marie returned. She looked a few pounds lighter but still had her usual sour glare and sharp manner. She didn't mention why she had gone when she resumed my lessons.

After class one evening, as I waited for my parents, I ask a boy who also studied piano about the teacher's unexplained absence.

"You don't know?" says the pudgy, tow-haired boy smugly, staring at me in disgust as if I were the lone creature on earth who didn't know.

"She went to the looney bin because she's crazy," he blurts.

"Oh," I giggle.

"Miss Marie *is* looney tunes," I sing song, unaware of the teacher listening behind the kitchen door.

When the boy leaves with his father, Miss Marie shoots into the studio like a test flight from Cape Canaveral. She plucks a gray folding chair from a corner of the room, drags it across the scratched wood floor, and plops it beside me.

"Let me tell you what it's like," she cackles, her enormous flashing eyes boring into mine like a plumber's snake.

I lower my head, stare at my shoelaces, and tap my tennis shoes against the grainy floor.

"They lock you up in your room at night, but you can't sleep because the others wail, scream, and moan. They feed you strange pills. During the day, you wander the halls mumbling to yourself with nothing to do or anyone to talk to. Outsiders can't visit."

She pauses to catch her breath and stares at the ceiling.

I squirm and peek at the ancient wall clock above the piano—10 after 7, my parents are late. I close my eyes, swallow hard to ease the growing lump in my throat.

"Listen!" she orders sharply.

"The guards steal your cigarettes. They sometimes tie your arms and legs and strap you to a table."

At the mention of straps and being tied to a table, I groan and jump briskly from the chair, which thuds to the floor.

"That's enough," says Mister Anthony, his face a shade paler than usual, who has materialized out of thin air.

"You are scaring her. She's just a child."

"She's old enough to call me loony," the agitated woman retorts with a frown and twists her skinny neck toward me.

She was about to go on when headlights rippled across the worn floorboards. I hear the familiar chug of my Dad's 12-year-old Chevy engine. Scooping up my music books from the floor, I bolt toward the wood screen door, which bangs shut loudly, and sprint across the yard to the car.

Safely ensconced in the sedan's backseat, breathless, my heart galloping, I spit out what had just happened, leaving out the part about my calling the teacher "looney tunes."

"Está loca," Mom huffs. She's crazy.

Dad nods, releases the brake, and eases the car onto Laurel Street, five minutes from our home.

"I'm never going back," I shouted as a voice in my head whispered: *watch out, or you'll end up in the loony bin just like your piano teacher.*

* *

I never told my parents, teachers, school nurse, or church minister about the panics and exaggerated fears. They were my secret, a private shame. You dare not admit your faults or insecurities when you feel like an alien creature in a strange land, like a hapless puppy desperate to fit in with new owners.

Specific topics were taboo for my immigrant family—a girl's first period, dating, sex—before and after marriage—giving birth and dying. None of my immediate relatives discussed why my grandfather died, where he'd gone, or why I would never see him again. Three days later, when it was time to inter him, my young cousins and I were not allowed to go to his burial—which could have worsened my childhood fears or allowed me to say *adios, abuelo,* goodbye.

Occasionally as a child, I sometimes complained about a stomachache from eating a green mango, the sharp pains in my legs, nightmares, and my heart thumping for no reason. Mom would wave me away with a manicured hand.

"Nervios," she harrumphed.

Nerves were the catch-all phrase for any illness without an identifiable cause. After ordering me to go outside and play with my sisters, she returned to mopping the front porch or making *sofrito* for black bean soup.

Locura, madness, was not mentioned or talked about in my family. It was far too dangerous to admit you, a child, or a relative might be losing their mind.

For most immigrants, insanity is seen as a dangerous sign of weakness, a black stain on the family's future, and a potentially ruinous condition.

Why add mental illness—we didn't even know the term then— to the already long list of foreign traits that set us apart from the happy and well-adjusted ordinary American families we watched on Leave it to Beaver and the Partridge Family? I convinced myself that the aberrant fears, jumbled thoughts, and out-of-body experiences would pass.

I told myself, piensa en el futuro, think of the future, the needs of your poor parents and your younger sisters. *Our survival depends on pretending we are okay.*

Other conditions of the mind—postpartum depression, anxiety, panic attacks, bipolar disorder, mania—were not included in our immigrant vocabulary.

Unused to or unfamiliar with modern psychology and psychiatry, recent immigrants sometimes turn to unconventional rituals and superstitions from the old country or spiritual beliefs like Santeria in Cuba to deal with emotional or mental illness, just as my mother and her sisters sometimes did. More than half the population of the island is believed to practice Christianity and Afro-Cuban spirituality. Santeria, brought to Cuba by slaves from Nigeria and West Africa in the 17th and 18th centuries, imbues most aspects of life on the Caribbean island. After the conquest, Spanish priests intent on converting the slaves to Catholicism slyly converged Christian and African deities to create a new syncretic belief system.

Some Santeros blame disturbances of the mind on evil supernatural forces, a curse, or a magic spell known as *bilongo.*

A family legend is that *mal de ojo,* the evil eye, caused the death of my aunt Carmen's two children, a girl, age five, and a boy when he was eleven months old.

The boy was born healthy, but when he was about six months, he began to shriek inconsolably for hours, refused his mother's breast, and shriveled like a prune. The doctor was baffled. Nothing was physically wrong with the boy. His mother switched him to cow's milk, which the boy spit out, and then tried goat's milk. He took a few swallows and refused the bottle. He grew weaker by the day and died a month before he turned one. The child is buried in our family plot, where, a few years later, his sister, who didn't make it past age five, suffered a similar fate. My obstinate grandfather refused to visit the children while they were alive or attend their funerals. He never forgave their mother, who ran away to marry a Santeria priest at age sixteen. Some relatives blamed the children's deaths on Bilongo.

Back then, a common belief on the island was that newborns were especially vulnerable to evil spells from jealous or malicious people. Mothers pinned tiny talismans on a baby's top to guard against mal de ojo. So did my mother. I recall a story she often told of the time she carried me to a verbena, a county dance, at the white's only community club. I was a few months old then, and my mother's elder sister, Zoraida, came along to chaperone. The story, which I relate now, may explain why Mom agreed to take me to see a babalao, a Santeria high priest, for a spiritual cleansing when I was nine or ten, and we lived in Tampa.

* *

Guira de Melena, Cuba
1952

Fleshy arms pressed against the iron bars of an open window, Cuca and Tomasa peer inside the dance hall where the Saturday afternoon verbena is just starting.

In their white shifts and timeworn chancletas, the mulatas squeeze their narrow faces between the bars to peek at the musicians who strum the first few chords of a popular Beny Moré tune on their tres guitars. They stare at the neatly dressed couples who amble arm in arm to the dance floor, where their well-shod feet twitch in anticipation of the frisky mambo about to start.

Childhood friends from barrio La Cachimba, the women inhale deeply to catch the occasional whiff of cheap cologne and Bacardi rum emanating from the room.

Their obsidian eyes sparkle with excitement as they banter about the goings on inside.

"Look at those skinny calves teetering on five-inch heels," chuckles Tomasa and points to a short blonde in a tight red sheath. The woman's lips shine like rubies, and her white cheeks are smudged with rouge the size of Spanish medallions.

"How can she walk in those?" she laughs, "much less dance?"

"Si, si," nods Cuca, clucking her tongue. "And that dress! It reveals every curve Dios santo gave her."

Not one to be outdone by her friend's spicy comment, Tomasa, who is six inches shorter and has cinnamon-colored skin, unlike her chocolate-skinned friend, points to another woman with a revealing neckline.

"If it were deeper, you'd see to the bottom of Havana harbor," she chortles and cups a hand over her mouth to whisper in her friend's ear: "In their homemade dresses copied from Gringo magazines, they think they're high society."

Cuca guffaws. "They're guajiras, country gals, just like us."

"And take a good look at the men," she adds.

"Half-starved and not a kilo in their pocket, but decked out in their one guayabera, their cheeks nicked from a once-a-week shave."

As the friends giggle, something inside catches their hawk-like eyes—a young woman with blonde cascading curls at the entrance to the dance hall. She is no older than 20, wears a cotton dress hanging loosely over her round belly, and carries a pink bundle. She hesitates for a few seconds, then steps cautiously inside the jammed room and walks toward an empty corner of the dance floor. An older woman is like a shadow behind her.

"What's she carrying?" Cuca blurts.

"A baby, of course," Tomasa says.

"No way. It's gotta be a doll," Cuca pronounces. "Look at the porcelain face and arms. I saw a doll just like it once in a window of El Encanto in Havana."

"No seas tonta," retorts Tomasa. "Don't be silly. I know a baby when I see one. It's sleeping."

As the women continue arguing, the blonde with the bundle and her dark-haired companion sit on two empty straight-back chairs ten feet away from an open window.

"I'm going to find out!" Cuca whispers to Tomasa.

"Señora, come over here," she calls above the music and fast-paced conversation.

The blonde glances at Cuca and shrugs, and the older woman scowls.

During a break in the music, Cuca tries again; this time, she hisses loudly and makes a calling motion with her hand.

The blonde stares then rises from her chair and approaches the window. The other woman follows like her sentry.

"Que quieres?" asks the blonde curtly. "What is it you want?"

Cuca smiles and points to the bundle the woman carries.

"It's a doll, verdad?" she asks.

Tomasa interrupts.

"Don't listen to my friend. She's a boba, a ninny. It's real, a baby, right?"

The blonde smiles and gazes at the pink parcel pressed to her chest.

"Of course she's real," she laughs. "Unless I was dreaming during the nine months I carried her in my belly."

Cuca's lips quiver: she seems about to cry.

"I don't believe it. May I touch her?" she asks softly.

"Of course."

The mulatta extends a shivering hand over the swaddled bundle and strokes the pallid tiny arm, then caresses the rosy-cheeked face. The child opens her turquoise blue eyes and smiles as she does this.

"Linda.", coos Cuca. Pretty.

"Preciosa," clucks Tomasa.

"Let's go," the older woman barks, grabs the younger woman's elbow, and drags her away from the window.

"Why?" protests the blonde.

"They're witches," the older woman hisses.

"Santeras looking for a chance to cast Bilongo on a newborn. Best beware."

* *

A few years later—I was two or three—Aunt Carmen took me to a Santeria ceremony at a friend's home without telling my mother.

The scene is vivid as a colorized photograph. I cling to my aunt's hand as we join a circle of men, women, and children. A barefoot black woman, face dripping sweat, dances in the center. Her huge hips sway, and her shoulders jiggle. The hypnotic pounding of African tambores entrances her. She appears possessed by a supernatural force directing her quivering fleshy body, her violently jerking limbs, and the contortions of her face. She utters guttural sounds in an unrecognizable language.

I am too young to understand that I am witnessing a Santeria initiation ceremony called *poner santo*, where an Afro-Cuban deity descends from another realm and temporarily overtakes the initiate's body, soul, and mind. Believers say this santo becomes their life-long totem, offering protection, advice, and guidance.

No matter that I don't know what is happening, the woman's undulating movements transfix me, her tongue clicking against her ivory teeth, the strange syllables erupting like volcanoes from her bright red lips.

When the throbbing drum rhythm ends and the woman's gyrations stop, she collapses in a heap. My aunt says it's time to leave.

"No! I want to stay," I say, stomping one foot on the floor and letting go of her hand.

"It's over; we have to go," she winks.

"But if you don't tell your mother, we can come again."

Many years later, I mentioned the unforgettable ceremony to my mother. She was outraged.

"No sabia, I didn't know," she blurted.

"How could your aunt do that? Why did you wait so long to tell me?"

I offered no answer out of loyalty to my tia Carmen's independent, unconventional spirit.

* *

In fifth grade, my teacher Mrs. Rodríguez, who was Cuban like us, noticed something was wrong with me. I squirmed in my chair, chattered nonstop with schoolmates, and disrupted her math and grammar lessons. After I interrupted her one too many times, she marched me to the front of the class and slapped my palm with a ruler twelve times. The punishment worked for a while. But when I stabbed the boy sitting behind me with a pencil—he pulled my braid—she ordered me to see the principal, who suspended me from school for three days.

One afternoon, Mom arrived outside the classroom after the bell rang. The teacher invited her inside and locked the door; I waited in the hall, ear pressed to the glass panel in the heavy wood. I heard muffled sounds.

On the stroll home, my mother seemed withdrawn, and I didn't ask questions.

She waved me over to the kitchen sink a week later after dinner. "Put on your shoes," she ordered. "We're going out."

How strange. We never went out on school nights without my dad and sisters.

"Where are we going?"

"No preguntes, don't ask," she whispered so my father, ensconced like a spider in his brown recliner watching *Sanford and Son* on the black-and-white TV, couldn't hear her. I have no idea where she told him we were going.

"You'll see," she sighed, a touch of conspiracy in her lilting voice. She spirited me out the door to a friend's waiting car.

We pulled up to a dilapidated bungalow in a poorer section of our immigrant barrio. The house had a wide front porch decorated in white imitation Corinthian columns, typical of 19th-century cigar worker houses. As we climbed onto the shabby porch, tiptoeing around the broken floorboards, and approached the screen door, I caught a whiff of *agua de violeta*, violet water, which Mom sprinkled on my hair after washing it.

A man with outsized biceps and gleaming obsidian-black skin appeared behind the screen. His chest and arm muscles bulged from a sleeveless white cotton undershirt, just like what Dad wore after work. A thick gold chain with a four-inch pendant shaped like a lion dangled from his wide perspiring neck. He clenched an unlit cigar between his yellow teeth. The fat stub reminded me of a brown insect. With a wave of his hand and a bow of his head, he invites us inside.

"*Buenas noches*," he says in a deep baritone that sounds friendly yet ominous.

"I've been waiting for you."

I cover my mouth with my hand and gasp. The man is a babalao.

Mom has brought me to a high priest for a *limpieza*, a ritual cleansing. No longer scared; I am intrigued. Perhaps this man, whose business is to lift curses, grant wishes, and heal those afflicted with cancer, heartache, or baffling mental maladies, can cure me.

He politely begs my mother's pardon and requests that she wait in the living room, then guides me through a curtained doorway into a separate room. This room is no larger than a one-car garage, dim, hot, humid, and suffused with the musky smell of stale cigar smoke and decaying flowers. A small altar wedged in a corner is decorated with an assortment of objects: a row of cowrie shells, a coconut pod, several stones, a black pipe, an unpeeled *malanga* used for soups and stews, a minuscule glass container of rice, a miniature vial filled with honey-colored liquid next to a bottle of Bacardi. I recognize the wilting orange and yellow flowers in a vase propped behind a two-foot statue of La Caridad del Cobre, Cuba's patron saint. They are marigolds, *flores de muertos*, common at wakes and funerals, and ran alongside my grandparents' house where I played and sometimes hid from Mom and my aunts.

He points an index finger to a waist-high bed and asks me to remove my clothes. "Wrap this around your torso," he says gravely, handing me a white sheet.

When he turns to face the wall, I fumble with the homemade button-holes of my white cotton blouse, unzip my pleated skirt, slip off my under-pants, and remove my shoes and cotton socks. I fold each one and neatly place them on top of my loafers on the floor beside me. The tidy pile reminds me of dunes on the Causeway beach where Dad almost drowned once. Unlike Mom, whose idea of swimming is to stay in one spot near shore no more profound than two-feet deep—to keep her blonde hair-sprayed beehive intact—Dad, who is not a strong swimmer, prefers the deeper water and often swims laps for 10 or 15 minutes until he grows tired and returns to the shoreline.

That day the sea was unusually rough following a mighty afternoon downpour that cracked open the heavens and spit lightning for an hour, and halted abruptly. Relentless five and six-foot waves churned the brackish water; the undertow was unusually fierce. We watched from shore as Dad's head bobbed on the water and then disappeared under a crashing wave, only to remerge briefly and disappear with each successive wave.

A family friend who was with us, Gladys, noticed Dad was flailing. A good swimmer with muscular forearms and a Barbie Doll waist, she swam out, used her red fingernails to dig into the flesh of his chest, yanked him from beneath the water, and dragged him to shore. Lying motionless on the sand, Dad vomited green puke, the color of his face. At the same time, Mom fluttered her arms above his bruised, rigid body like a startled seagull repeating *alabao, alabao*, my, oh my, until Dad, with a sheepish grin on his bluish lips, sat up and said *no fue nada*, it was nothing. *Estoy bien*, I'm fine. I was sad when we lost touch with Gladys after she divorced Pepín, her husband, and moved in with a lesbian girl-friend—*un escandalo*, scandalous, according to my parents.

The man approaches and hovers beside me after I've tucked the bed sheet like a mummy around my body. I shiver, although the room is sweltering.

He rearranges the sheet around my torso, exposing my skinny arms and legs.

"Acuestate, lie down and close your eyes," he says, bending close to my face. I smell the garlic on his breath, shut my eyes, and try not to breathe. A metallic taste fills my mouth and throat. I smell something sweet and woodsy, like smoke from my grandfather's puros.

His heavy hands stroke my body, and he begins to chant slow, guttural, incomprehensible words that, to me, sound like gibberish.

"Oni no iku, obi no aro mo ku ko. Oni no Ku, obi no aro mo ku ko..."

He varies his pitch, now high, now low, the words are strange, but for a few, I recognize—Ochún, Yemayá, Changó, deities I have heard in family conversations and Cuban songs.

He rubs an oily substance over my limbs in deft, even strokes. The oil smells like the cocoa butter Dad rubs on my stomach when it hurts.

"Iya ye kuma kue yu mao! iya ye kuma kue yu mao! iya ye kuma kue yu mao!"

I half-open my eyes to see what he's doing.

"Close your eyes," he says gruffly. "You are not allowed to see."

I shut them. *I will focus on breathing like I do when I am about to faint.*

My breathing is ragged and comes in puffs that float like smoke rings toward the ceiling. I float up there, too, my body suspended in an inky cloud of smoke. I look down and watch the babalao's deft hands stroke my limbs. I hear crying.

I am asleep in a bedroom of my grandparent's home in Güira, no longer on a massage table in Tampa. I am four. Abuelo's body lies on a table twenty feet from where I sleep. I feel pressure on the back of my head. A hand pushes my face into the pillow. Something grips my forearm, pinning my right arm behind my back. A sinister presence behind me restrains my legs. Like a blindfolded fighter, I squirm and punch with my still-free left arm at the empty air.

I can't breathe. *Me muero.* I am dying.

I stop struggling, and the heavy hand suddenly lets go of my head.

"If you say a word, I'll kill you," the evil presence whispers and is gone.

I gulp for air like a goldfish removed from the water.

A shrill chorus of cicadas resonates inside the room. Someone sneezes.

"Open your eyes. You can dress now," the man says.

I stand up and feel a pounding sensation against my eardrums. My feet feel like cardboard boxes against the floorboards.

I grab the table's edge to steady myself, take a few steps toward the pile on the floor, bend down, pick up my clothes one at a time, and start to dress slowly as if I were moving underwater: blouse, skirt, underpants. I sit on the floor and pull on my socks and shoes.

When the man reappears, he draws aside the flowered curtain over the door. Mom is there, biting her lip, wringing her hands. She gives me a weak smile and takes my hand. "Are you crying?" she says, brushing my cheek with her hand. I shake my head no.

"*Vamos.* Let's go."

As we walk toward the screen door, she plucks a creased five-dollar bill from her plastic purse and places it on the babalao's oily palm. The night outside is balmy. I gaze up past the harsh light of a solitary lamppost. Salmon-pink-and-silver streaks pierce the inky sky. No moon in sight. As we climb into the friend's waiting car, the man shouts a final instruction.

"Place a fresh glass of water, half full, under the bed at night," he says. "It will dispel any remaining demons."

I follow his command for a few nights—I figure it can't hurt— then forget about the dusty water glass under the bed. Mom doesn't mention it again.

A few years ago, I dared to ask her about our surreal visit to the babalao. She denied it had happened. I do not challenge her, nor do I hold this and other moments of amnesia against her. She was a distraught mother at a loss as to how to help her disturbed child. Even though it went against her Christian faith, Santería was home.

CHAPTER 3

THE KARMA OF EXILE

*"I have nothing against nostalgia, so long as we
acknowledge it is a pacific form of rage."*

—Eliseo Alberto.

Humberto, a Cuban exile I met in El Paso, helped me understand the spiritual and psychic split felt by exiles. He materialized at my university office door on a cold January day like a Chihuahua desert *grillo* seeking warmth. He wore a light-gray cashmere coat that reached down to his ankles, two sizes too big for his small frame. It reminded me of the carapace of an exotic insect.

"Hola, profesora," he shouted, shoving a soft hand with manicured nails toward me.

I guessed his nationality before he mentioned it because of his informal, friendly manner, rapid run-on Spanish, and how he waved his arms as if they were exclamation marks.

Humberto never revealed his age, but I guessed he was in his 70s because he shared details about his pre-exile life in Havana. At age thirteen, he left his "Cuba querida," beloved Cuba, from Havana harbor the day Batista absconded. A rich uncle owned the ferry boat line that carried him to Fort Lauderdale, where he had some family. Another uncle had been a Supreme Court Justice in the 40s and 50s. His parents owned several plantations, a big fancy Colonial manor house in swanky Miramar, and a summer house on Varadero Beach. He and his family were on a first-name basis with the Batista clan.

"What brought you to the U.S.-Mexico border with Mexico" I inquired.

He told me he and his third wife had moved from Austin so he could finally finish his medical studies across the river in Juarez. He had begun training in Spain fifty years earlier but was kicked out because of his poem calling the dean an *enano*, a dwarf, which in Spanish rhymes with *decano*. It had circulated widely among the professors and student body and caused a ruckus. He had noticed some friction with his Juarez professors and wanted my advice.

"I'm not sure how to help you," I replied, "but I am happy to talk over a *cafecito*."

After several cups of coffee that tasted like *agua de chinga*—my mom's colorful description for watery, tasteless Maxwell House coffee—I learned his backstory.

He left Cuba after the revolution and went to Spain, where he'd become an international banker, made, and then lost, a million bucks in the stock market, then immigrated to the U.S. where he had done a bit of *inteligencia*—intelligence work—for the U.S. government. I thought it best not to probe.

With his sly smile, sharp wit, and twinkling brown eyes, Humberto was a rascal and charmer.

After I got to know him better, he confided that within minutes of our meeting, he recognized the "Cubana guajira" in me.

"All I had to do was scratch the surface," he grinned broadly.

Our shared heritage, and the brotherly confianza we developed, prompted me to ask if he would be willing to read some chapters in my memoir.

"My pleasure," he smiled.

One week later, he offered to buy me lunch. We met one spring afternoon at a crowded Italian restaurant less than a mile from the interstate highway that divides El Paso from Ciudad Juarez.

"You get a lot of meal for your money in this place," he chuckled and guided me to a square table covered by a red-checkered plastic tablecloth and a red glass candle holder in the center.

After our lunch—spaghetti, meatballs, and iced tea for me; spaghetti with clam sauce and a carafe of Chianti for Humberto—he handed me a manila folder.

"Open it," he grinned.

Inside were four single-spaced typewritten pages with blue pen scrawls on the margins.

"Read it," he beamed, excited as a schoolboy who had received an "A" on a test.

"OK," I said, held my breath, and began to read.

The title was *Unqualified, Unsolicited and Unwarranted Psychiatric Evaluation of a Writer, for Whose Forgiveness I Beg.*

I glanced at Humberto, who nodded and gazed out the restaurant door to the parking lot.

Little girl whose security is shattered by a new, hostile environment when forcefully adapting to the new realities of exile in an alien world withdraws as a snail to maintain her sanity, which she barely manages to do throughout life at a substantial psychological cost. She only finds security within the walls of her dwellings but immediately loses it every time she must leave them for another experience."

I blink and look up. Humberto sips his third glass of wine.

"There's quite a bit of truth here," I say, blushing.

"Go on," he urges.

Although it triggered the condition, the problem is not limited to the split from her native Cuba. It returns as an unwelcome, fearsome, terrible phantom every time her frail, difficulty-built security is broken by a compulsory move to a new and therefore, always-hostile place. The patient (patient?) is hopelessly insecure and incapable of making her new habitats adapt to her, so instead, intimidated by them, she tries to cope as best she can, with the accompanying psychological cost. Even when empowered and protected by family, her own intellectual and excellent professional level, and relative wealth, her psychological condition requires time in order to achieve minimal stability. Personality being extremely stable, she will always be highly insecure and, probably, will only unify her double sense of identity if she were to return to her native origins, which she so strongly identifies with.

I pause again as Humberto drinks another mouthful of wine.

"You think I must return to Cuba to regain my sense of security?" I ask.

"Keep reading," he nudges.

The patient is like a symbiotic hybrid, in which both sides overlap and simultaneously, reject and feed off each other. However, she is really not much different from the rest of us Cubans, who for many years have not been able to return to the land where we first saw light."

"Symbiotic hybrid?" I chuckle. "I may use that in my book."

Humberto looks drowsy and leans toward me.

I shift uncomfortably in my chair when I come to the last part of his evaluation of my psyche.

You are an extremely sensitive person, one able 'to feel' the differences between your natural (Cuban) and your American acquired pragmatic and defensive selves. You have suffered most of your life from pre-morbid paranoid schizophrenia. Humberto has crossed out the "you" in this sentence and written "we" in blue ink above it.

I strike the table hard with my fist. Several patrons stare.

"You've explained *me*," I exclaim.

"My pleasure," he says, waving at the frumpy waitress for the check.

He lowers his voice when she takes his credit card and walks away.

"You're not so weird after all. You are Cuban and only Cuban; your acquired self, like mine, has developed only for the pragmatic need for survival."

"That's just part of it," I protest, looking at the yellow streaks of sunlight pouring through the open door.

Humberto frowns. His light brown eyes twinkle like Christmas tree lights. He adjusts his collar.

"You are not searching for home, Zita," he whispers.

As he says this, an image from *The Wizard of Oz* flashes through my mind: Dorothy has returned to Kansas and wakes from her tornado-induced coma. Toto is asleep beside her; Auntie M and her companions from Oz—Tin Man, Cowardly Lion, and Scarecrow—now men in workaday clothes—hover above her bed.

"What's home?" I implore.

"You have always been in Cuba," he says softly as if cooing to a newborn, "while just renting in the U.S."

I rise and place a light kiss on his cheek.

"Perhaps you're right," I say, my voice choking.

"I've got to go; got a class to teach," I say, grab my purse and stride out the door into the bright desert sun.

* * *

I had a dream once about another Humberto, an uncle who married my mother's younger sister, Caridad. He was the movie-star handsome, ambitious son of small-town grocers who immigrated to my town from the Spanish Canary Islands in the early 1900s. His merchant parents thumbed their noses at their guajiro neighbors. After Humberto married my tia, they moved from our poverty-stricken village to the capital, where he became a prosperous coffee salesman, able to purchase an imported late-model Chevrolet and a Tiffany lamp at the fancy department store in old Havana.

The chandelier hung from the living room ceiling of a modern concrete block house he bought *al contado*, all cash. It was a short walk to his employer, the Regil Coffee Company, a long low rectangular building that still exists, as does my aunt and uncle's former home, now head-quarters of the neighborhood Comité Por La Defensa de la Revolucíon, Committee for the Defense of the Revolution. I never had the heart to tell this to my relatives, who were fierce anti-Communists and abhorred Fidel.

In my dream, Humberto lays on a plush and expensive Sealy Posture-pedic mattress and says wistfully, "The mattresses were better in Cuba." This curious dream belies the cruel reality of exile for most immigrants to America who flee poverty, crime, political disasters, and now climate change in their countries of origin. No matter the dire conditions forcing them to leave, the homeland is always finer in their imaginations. When I was a kid, a special treat for my family was a trip to eat tropical-flavored ice creams a few miles from our West Tampa home. My parents would bemoan that the papaya, guanabana, and guava from Cuba were juicier, sweeter, the real deal.

Despite his hard-won American prosperity, my uncle—and most Cubans who left for the U.S. after the revolution—was unable or unwilling to shake off his enduring nostalgia for the sounds, tastes, scents, and warm tropical sea breezes of his birthplace. The immigrant's mind is always *allá*, back there.

Before these relatives left for Florida in the mid-60s, Humberto served nine months of a five-year sentence at the Combinado del Este prison. This dreaded, dangerous place dates to Spanish Colonial times. He was accused of committing the counterrevolutionary act of selling sugar-adulterated coffee to unsuspecting customers. His wife, my tia, insists a jealous co-worker framed him.

While a prisoner, he was forced to remove heavy furniture from the confiscated three-and-four-story Vedado mansions of wealthy Cubans who fled. When he was released from prison, he was a bedridden, pain-wracked skeleton, his spine dislocated, his legs crippled; his wife and daughter had to feed and bathe him for a year.

After the family arrived in Tampa, my uncle opened a butcher shop that expanded beyond his imagination—Cubans consume daily quantities of beef and pork with their staple black beans and rice. Planeloads of new immigrants arrived in Tampa each month.

Later, he invested in real estate and gained a reputation as a philanthropist, giving away scholarships to recent arrivals to study medicine or go to law school. Many of the young people he helped came to his funeral when he died of cancer in his late 70s.

Before he died, my tio kept a locked safe with cash and jewels beneath the marble floors of his custom-built suburban ranch house. One time, during a wedding party at his home, he paraded around the dome-enclosed swimming pool wearing a moth-eaten ill-fitting coat and fur cap—clothing he'd worn when he landed penniless in Florida. He laughed as he showed off his ancient attire to the guests. Funny. Perhaps he wanted to remind us of his hard-scrabble exile beginnings and how he and his wife had worked hard and built a new life in America. Despite their newfound success, they never forgave or forgot the loss of their previous material wealth—his good-paying job, their three-bedroom concrete house, my aunt's sewing machines, and their Chevy sedan. Unlike other exiles, they refused to return to their homeland, even when the political climate made it possible.

My dad poured his nostalgia into ten-line rhyming poems called *décimas*, a poetic tradition that dates to medieval Spain. His décimas brimmed with melancholy. He crooned about his innocence and youth on the farm, how he missed Florinda, his dead, long-suffering mother, and the extraordinary beauty of his then-novia, my fair-haired, blue-eyed mother Olga, who looked like a 40s screen star.

He did well in the U.S. for a barely literate guajiro who worked for a dollar all day on a sugar plantation owned by a wealthy hacendado. In Tampa, Dad learned English at night school and purchased a shotgun house in an immigrant barrio, which he and my mother paid off in ten years at $50 a month. When he suffered a stroke in his early fifties and couldn't return to his plumbing job, he bought a shiny used Ford truck for $7000 cash and continued to do what he had learned to love in America: laying pipe and repairing pipe leaks and unclogging toilets. He even convinced Mom to build a two-car garage for his precious truck and his pristine ten-year-old lime-green Chevy sedan.

"I wish I'd never left Cuba," he confided a year or two before he died.

"Porque, why?"

"My brothers, my land," he said softly, his eyes misty. He recalled a recent dream in which his brothers, Mario and Corucho, showed up outside his bedroom window as young boys and invited him outside to play.

Dad never betrayed his true self. He remained a guajiro poet, a farmer's son, the shoeless boy who sucked on raw sugarcane, ate bird's eggs from nests, and was born on a kitchen table. He told his friends that he gave up rhyming and guitar strumming after he married Mom, and his uncle warned him away from the troubadour life.

"A poet is a dreamer, a vagabond, or a clown," Uncle Mino said. Mom says that once after they were married, Dad came home at dawn after a night of carousing and crooning with his poet buddies. He was woozy and thick-headed from too much rum and a lack of sleep.

She was furious.

"Make your choice," she yelled. "It's me or your guitar."

Sometimes he'd say to whoever would listen that after he moved to Tampa, he parked his guitar in a corner and vowed never to play again.

This wasn't entirely true.

Sometimes, he'd slip out from under my mom's eagle eye and spend a few hours at a neighbor's house singing and reciting poems.

He continued to write décimas—one each time a daughter married or gave birth to a grandchild. Most touched on ordinary life events, and some were funny, like one about a friend with a crooked toe that popped out of his shoe.

* *

Ever cautious and risk-averse, Dad once took a poker gamble at my mom's insistence. As we waited in Guira for our exit papers, Mom cajoled him into going to Tampa alone to test the waters.

At first, he refused, but when my mother's aunt Carmen, a widow who lived in Tampa, said she would pay for his one-way ticket, he had no choice but to agree.

My tia Carmen was complex, no-nonsense, angry, sharp-tongued, and crafty. She hated men—most probably because the older man she married, a barber of Spanish descent who immigrated to Tampa, gave her syphilis which made her baren.

Despite her prickly nature, my starving family would not have immigrated without her help.

As soon as Dad arrived alone—his pockets empty and carrying a battered suitcase—on the doorstep of Carmen's boarding house across from a 19th-century cigar factory on Armenia Avenue., she recited the house rules: no long showers, no snacks between meals, the refrigerator was off-limits at all hours, she was not his servant or laundress. And no loafing. He was there to find a job quickly and go to work.

Dad shared a back bedroom with my mother's dreamy, ne'er-do-well brother, Orlando, who had immigrated to Tampa a few years earlier.

One night as my father lay in his twin bed next to his brother-in-law and stared at the ceiling, he heard Carmen rattling pots in the kitchen and muttering—*asqueroso... muerto de hambre... guajiro pordiosero...*

"Who is she talking about when she says, 'good for nothing...starving... filthy...country bumpkin.'"

"You, of course," laughed Orlando, who leaned out the window as he puffed on a Marlboro. No smoking inside the house was another decree.

"She's called me worse," he chuckled.

"Why do you think she rushes into the bathroom with a pail, mop, and jug of Clorox whenever we finish showering?"

She hates us."

Dad turned toward the wall next to his bed and fixed his eyes on two thumb size photographs of his young daughters that he kept in his empty wallet. He longed to return home but was determined to get up each morning, put on his pants, and work at the glass factory, not for his sake but theirs. He would ignore the aunt's onerous house rules, bad temper, and sharp tongue.

Already uncertain and despondent, two incidents exacerbated his homesickness—an accident at work that sliced open his right palm, followed by a raid by immigration agents demanding to see his work permit. Dad lied that he had one and promised to return with it the following morning.

Three weeks later, penniless, humiliated, and in deep depression, he showed up outside my mother's door with a vow to *nunca*, never leave home again. Mom turned silent as a sphinx, and Dad took to bed for days, then weeks.

As the days passed by and my comatose Dad displayed no desire to get up, my no-nonsense tia Zoraida once again saved the day; her frequent gifts of money and food had helped sustain us before.

She flung open the bedroom door, blocked the doorway with her spindly frame, and like Jesus before Lazarus, commanded Dad to rise.

"Stop acting like a *mamón*," Tia barked. "You have a wife and two girls to feed. Debts to pay."

She had good news. "I spoke to the *capataz* at the *finca*, and he wants you back. Your old truck and job are waiting for you."

Humiliated by her harsh but necessary words, my father got up, jammed *a sombrero de guano on his head*, and scrambled back behind the wheel of his hauling truck. Occasionally he was required to chauffeur his exacting and explosive boss, Benito Remedios, to Havana for business meetings or to check the ongoing work at his far-flung plantations. Dad smiled again, joking and playing with his daughters, just as in the old days. He shared stories and new décimas with his poet friends.

Life had returned to normal, his immediate horizon clear.

He returned from work one day to find Mom, legs splayed and hands on her hips, waiting for him on the front porch. She smiled broadly, eyes twinkling like a summer meadow full of lightning bugs.

"We are going to Florida," she said breathlessly, her body swaying and her heels bouncing on the floorboards.

"Our immigration papers are approved. The next step is to visit the moneylender to borrow money for airfare."

My dad's face turned white as the sun-bleached jawbone of a dead cow; a lump large as a softball blocked his windpipe.

"No, *me voy*, I am not leaving," declared my mild-mannered father, with an emphasis on "I" and "no."

Mom huffed and held her knuckles like a prizefighter in a boxing ring. She fixed her flashing blue eyes on her husband's soft caramel-colored ones.

"That's what you think," she said in an icy tone.

"I'm leaving with or without you. And I'm taking the girls with me."

* * *

Is Cuba the home of memory and dreams I've wanted to return to or just a mirage? Can we go home again, and if we can't, where is home? Life as an exile sometimes feels like the after-death state of the Tibetan Bardo, described as an in-between, indeterminate, transitory place, a kind of no man's land—sort of the Christian hell.

After my drum teacher David's ritual cremation in Colorado, we performed rituals on his behalf for the following forty-nine days to help guide his spirit through the land of the bardo—a place said to be filled with terrifying visions and harsh, discordant sounds. The purpose of the ritual was to guide him through the bardo to help him reach the pure land of enlightenment. As a committed lifelong practitioner of the esoteric form of Buddhism called Dzogchen, I want to believe David attained nirvana.

Exile seems like existence without a proper home. It feels temporary, provisional, like the bardo or the Catholic purgatory. Some immigrants, like my parents, never transition to a new life. After they leave their native ground, they remain in a state of limbo, tethered to the illusion of return and regaining the lost home.

My parents lived in America for over five decades but have yet to embrace their new cultural reality fully.

Immigrants move forward looking backward, like the scene in a French movie where the heroine rides in the backseat of a racing car and faces back toward the rapidly receding roadway. I, too, focus on what I've lost, not what I have gained.

A dream I had captures this exile sense of floating without support or foundation like an astronaut—except those space explorers are tethered to oxygen from a mother ship. I am not. In the dream, I climb a stairway into the vast universe, past the moon and stars, toward far-flung galaxies with no fixed point in sight. I feel secure as I take one careful step up at a time. But the previous steps have disappeared when I turn my head to look behind. With every step up, the one I leave dissolves. I clutch an imaginary stair railing, terror roiling my body. I wake up breathless; my fists clenched, my face and chest covered in oceans of sweat. The dream is a metaphor. It reveals what I've always known: you can't go home again.

In truth, every human being is an exile from someplace, someone, something—a lost lover, a dead child, a home left abandoned or destroyed by water or fire, our mother's womb, which is our original exile. Life is *cambio*, change, continual loss. As much as we long for the illusory sense of safety we felt in our first home when it's gone, the lost home becomes a never healing wound or a phantom limb we think is still there.

I sleepwalked as a child in our house on St. John Street, where I spent most of my childhood until I married. The pitched roof cigar worker's bungalow is the closest thing to "home" I have experienced. My parents slept at the back of the house, next to the yellow and avocado green 60s-style rectangular kitchen that led to a leaky wood-and-aluminum addition where they made the tamales they sold for those few years.

I shared the front bedroom with one of my sisters. Dad says he once heard something rattling in the kitchen after everyone was asleep. He got up to check the source and found me standing at the back door, jiggling the doorknob, trying to get out. My eyes were wide open, and when Dad realized I was asleep, he led me back to my bed.

"Where were you trying to go?" he joked later, suppressing a laugh.

"There are no planes or boats back to Cuba."

Beneath the joke lay the harsh reality that there was no return, although Dad tried once in the mid-60s when he received a telegram from a sister in Cuba.

"Our mother is dead," it read. "It's too late to come."

Determined to at least witness his mother's burial, he made a few tearful phone calls to his family and explored the possibility of traveling to Havana through Jamaica or Canada—there were no direct U.S. flights to Cuba then. The cost was prohibitive. It was the first and only time I saw my father cry. A few years later, when my mother's mother died, there was no legitimate way to return for her funeral. After that, we learned of other deaths, births, baptisms, and weddings through letters and pictures that took a month or two or longer to reach us.

The ambivalent feeling of not belonging here or there (or anywhere) reminds me of a two-headed calf I once saw in a store window in downtown Ciudad Juarez. The tan-and-white stuffed calf was three feet tall. Its body was normal but for two perfectly formed heads. Four glassy eyes stared at me from behind the dusty display case. I shivered and thought, what a strange pitiable deformed creature. *Pobrecita.* Her Siamese heads are perpetually split, just as I am between Cuba and the U.S., *aquí y allá,* here and there. In this perpetual contradanza between two separated but joined heads, each twists, turns, tugs, and pulls, but the two heads are forever joined in health, sickness, and death. They have no choice but to travel through life conjoined.

Wherever we live, a perpetual sense of inauthenticity also haunts exiles. If the place we were born is our true home, then the adoptive place is pretense or vice versa. Favoring one is a betrayal of the other. *Quien soy?* Who am I? Best to equivocate.

My fragmented self appears in repetitive dreams of different houses and of particular spaces—attics, basements, and kitchens—inside places I've lived. These dwellings are carnival houses. They have scary, unexplored rooms of broken, distressed furniture and mountains of bric-a-brac. I tiptoe inside them, anxious about what I might find. One dream is of a tidy colonial house surrounded by park-like gardens; this house is near rising water that threatens to sweep it away. Another home has walls that are crumbling and full of menacing strangers. A particularly frightful dream is of an old woman dying inside an empty house, and I can't convince her to leave.

These spectral houses are never home. Neither are the ones where I've lived or might want to live. I scour real estate ads in places I visit—Georgia, New Jersey, and Santa Fe—hoping to find the perfect one. I never do.

During one of my meditations, I take an imaginative stroll through the many houses of my life and find them all wanting. There is the original family home in Guira, of course; various rental houses in West Tampa where we lived during our early immigrant years; the shotgun house my parents purchased; different apartments in Tampa when I was a young adult; a small second-floor attic apartment with a cute Romeo and Juliet balcony overlooking a tree-lined street in Miami; a four-bedroom 11th-floor apartment in Puerto Rico with views of the Caribbean and El Yunque; a red gabled house in Coral Gables where my daughter Miranda was born and I suffered the first of many depressions; a fixer-upper Colonial in Bethesda, Maryland—this one a frequent subject of my dreams—a Sunset Heights apartment near my university job in El Paso. This is my favorite; it was perched on top of a bald mountain from which I could see the sprawling city of Juarez, Mexico, and almost touch the telephone wires. When I looked out the bank of windows, it felt as if I were flying with the birds outside.

Even the West Tampa cañon, the bungalow where I lived longest as a child, felt incomplete like us, a bell missing a gong. It had an aluminum-covered pitched roof, a wide front porch where my sisters and I played in the sweltering summers, and wood slat walls. Ours was one of the thousands of similar houses built for Cuban and Italian cigar-factory immigrant workers in West Tampa and Ybor City in the late 19th and early 20th Century.

Our cañon had 1919 carved on the concrete driveway next to the porch and was less than eight blocks from the red brick Garcia y Vega cigar factory where my mother rolled cigars for a few years. My sisters and I jumped rope, played marbles, and plucked the back legs off grasshoppers in the driveway. We had two chickens and an aggressive rooster. After a neighbor complained about its crowing, I returned from school one day to find the rooster gone and asked Dad where it was. He said he'd given it away to a farmer. I'm sure the bird ended up in Mom's *sopa de pollo*, just like the chickens.

Over time we remodeled the house ourselves. We installed new aluminum windows and doors, and we covered the inside wood walls with planks of sheetrock and lowered the fourteen-foot ceilings—my sister and I raised the planks way above our heads with long wooden poles and held them there so Dad could nail the plasterboard to the ceiling beams. One family project was to cover the floors with beige vinyl tiles, and I spent hours over several weeks on my knees helping Dad glue them down. Later, we installed brown and tan shag carpeting in the bedrooms. Mom was proud of her modern yellow and avocado green appliances, a double oven, a cooktop, and a double-sided refrigerator from Sears.

After a pressure cooker of black beans exploded, smearing black crud over the ceiling and walls, we were able to have it repainted courtesy of the insurance company. Mom—who enjoyed rearranging tables, chairs, and sofas often—decided to divide the narrow room and hired a handyman to build a divider for the living room. Dad's carpenter friend made a four-foot *medio punto,* which resembled a white brick wall with an opening at the top for beach sand and plastic flowers. The separation was the focal point of family portraits, including one of me dressed in a baby-pink chiffon gown and beehive hairstyle just before leaving with a boy to the senior prom —my first and only date in high school. Despite the improvements and other renovations, the house remained a termite-infested shack, sweltering in summer and cold as a freezer in the winter. I always felt provisional inside its flimsy walls, just a ghost passing through.

Over the last twenty years, my abode has been a passive solar adobe in Southern New Mexico. Despite its charms, the house seems dark and dank; its roof sometimes leaks, and the rain leaves long streaks of orange mud along the walls. Sometimes I'm startled by squirrels or skunks padding across the flat roof and the thud of confused pigeons that crash into the broad windows. It, too, feels impermanent, and I tell friends I'm just a caretaker.

And yet moving from each house has felt like a personal death. Leaving them resurrects a too-precise memory of a four-year-old girl with golden curls riding in the back seat of a car that speeds through mud-caked streets past blooming hibiscus, red pepper shrubs, and giant skinny palm trees toward the airport. She is crying.

* * *

I have a few memories of our first departure in 1957. The clearest is of me, my sister, and my parents pressed against a plate glass window at the airport, waving goodbye to my sobbing grandmother, aunts, and cousins on the other side. But memory is crafty and imprecise. What we remember changes, disappears, and returns in reconstructed form.

For a long time, I conflated our departure in 1957 with the harrowing one in January 1959, as Batista fled at night and the rebels declared victory from their mountain hideouts. My brain may have conflated the two leave-takings because, in '59, I was older and more aware of what was happening outside. Also, the second departure was definitive. After we returned to Tampa after the revolution, Cuba remained inscrutable, a mystery and a blur for the following twenty years, like a faintly scented handkerchief tucked for a long time in a dresser drawer.

* * *

January 1959
Tampa, Florida

Mami totters at the top of the airplane stairs, gazing down at the shiny tarmac of Miami International Airport. It is midnight on a brisk January day, and an icy wind pierces our flimsy tropical clothes. My dad is beside her; my sister and I have paused a few steps behind them. We clutch life-size dolls and gifts from Los Reyes Magos during our family vacation to Cuba.

Mom wears five-inch heels and carries a bag of oranges from my grandparent's backyard. As she wobbles down the metal stairs on her spikes, the paper sack bursts; the oranges tumble like marbles down the steps one at a time and roll onto the smooth black landing strip.

My sister and I watch our parents scurry after the spinning orbs from the top of the airplane stairs. The scene unfolds like a film reel in slow motion. Mom and Dad scamper after the fruit, gleaming orbs spinning onto an edgeless blacktop universe. Our parents scoop up the rolling oranges as if they were family diamonds. Dad stuffs some in his pants pockets and Mom inside her shiny patent-leather purse. A tall woman in a pencil-thin skirt runs after them with a bag in one hand and helps collect the rest of the fruit. From our perch at the top of the airplane stairs, we watch as the blonde woman hands the sturdy bag to my dazed mother.

She wears a little blue cap above her blonde bouffant and has perfect lips like a Kewpie doll. They remind me of the red Habanero pepper I once plucked from a bush near my grandparent's house. The pepper looked like a Christmas ornament, and my mouth watered as I crammed it into my mouth, expecting it to taste sugar. Instead, fire scorched the tip of my tongue, throat, and windpipe. No matter how much water I drank—I must have asked Abuela for at least a dozen glasses that afternoon—quenched the tormenting thirst. I remember Abuela wanted to know why I was so thirsty. Embarrassed over my mistaking a pepper for candy, I shrugged and lied: "I don't know."

After retrieving the spinning oranges, the blonde woman waves my sister Olga and me down the metal stairs to join our parents on the tarmac. The tarmac resembles a precipice in a universe of unexplored planets, shooting stars, and black holes.

"Welcome to Florida," the stewardess coos as I run my tongue over dry lips.

* * *

The memory is flawed like a cracked piece of prized family China hidden in a back corner of an antique cupboard or torn stitches on a dress seam.

This arrival in Miami was in early '59 when Castro and his rebels declared victory over the corrupt Batista regime, crowds smashed gambling machines and parking meters, and the country said *adios* to U.S. interference. Like other innocents abroad who soon lose touch with current events in their home country, we returned to reunite with relatives and pay overdue debts to the grocer and moneylender. Instead, we walked into a revolution and a collapsed government. After the rebels reopened the airport and we could return to Florida, we lost sight of our relatives for two decades.

This was our true exile.

* * *

"Mami, remember when we landed here?" I inquired a few years ago.

"*Porque preguntas*, why do you ask?"

She knows I'm writing a memoir and gets a little testy when I ask about the past. I persist.

"Remember when the sack broke, and you dropped the oranges?"

Mom interrupts: "They were tamales," she corrects me.

I have always remembered oranges.

But, no, Mom insists they were tamales with *trocitos de puerco* from my grandmother's kitchen. Tamales are a Cuban staple like café con leche or black beans. I do not press. Mom remembers tamales. The sack will always contain citrus fruit from home in my mind and a symbol of the abandoned Latino heritage surrendered with our passports upon arrival in this country. There *are* oranges in Florida, after all, they just taste less sweet.

CHAPTER 4

BLACK TEARS
LÁGRIMAS NEGRAS

My mother blames Santeria for all the bad that happened to her and her sisters growing up, but I blame my grandfather. Abuelo guarded his four daughters as if they were prized hothouse orchids. He was typical of men back then—strict, domineering, *el macho de la pelicula*, the leading man, as they say in the movie world. He dictated what my mother and her sisters wore—nothing too tight or low cut—where they went—no dance halls or movies unless their mother chaperoned. Most importantly, he decided whom they dated and married. White men were his daughters' only romantic option: immigrants from the old country were preferable. Even light-skinned mulattos were forbidden love interests.

Although Abuelo was kind and protective of his grandchildren, he had authoritarian proclivities coursing through his tough Spanish veins. They say every action causes a reaction, sometimes good, sometimes bad. Buddhists call this karma. My grandfather's stubborn, controlling tendencies—most probably passed down from his father and grandfather—produced unfortunate consequences for his five children, especially his daughters, Olga, my mother, Caridad, Carmen, and Zoraida, the oldest, and his wife, Matilde, my meek, glum grandmother. His anger may have infected a grandson who terrorized my sister and me as children. This long-dead cousin also hurt others, physically and in other ways, although some relatives may deny it.

Matilde was a child of the old-world 19th-century patriarchy that kept women in their place, at home under their husband's rule and thumb. In those days, my grandfather decided all matters related to the children's discipline, education, and future. Abuela ensured they ate, bathed, wore clean clothes, and rested. She even washed, combed, and brushed the tangles from her daughters' waist-length hair well into their teenage years.

She was submissive about most things but not about *her cocina*. Like an imperious queen, she ruled the kitchen, the domain of feminine power inside homes in those long-ago pre-revolutionary days. The eight-by-ten-foot room at the back of the house with an earthen floor, a water spigot, and coal burning stove was off-limits to everyone, especially her daughters, who were desperate to learn her cooking secrets and stood outside at the kitchen window to sneak peeks as their mother slaved over the *fogón*.

"Go away," she barked, her eyes tearing from chopping onions on a pockmarked mango wood plank.

"You'll learn to cook soon enough once you are married."

Matilde was in her early fifties when I was born, an elf-like four-feet, five inches tall, with deep wrinkles like craters lining her forehead and cheeks. I remember she walked with her sad brown eyes glued to the floor and referred to my grandfather as *señor*, sir.

Her feet were so tiny that she wore a child's shoe size. She rarely laughed, and pictures show her with arms crossed against her flat chest and thin lips forming an upside-down U. The frown was to hide her missing front teeth, common among poor women from the countryside.

She prepared three meals daily, cleaned the house, and heated dozens of buckets of water daily for bathing and washing clothes. She mended, washed, starched, and ironed her husband's khaki police uniforms and her daughter's cotton underwear, the sheets, towels, and pillowcases. It must have been a relief for her aching back and sore feet when her daughters grew old enough to use a coal iron without setting themselves ablaze, which sometimes happened. In those pre-electric times, it wasn't unusual for women to suffer burns from flying sparks from the charcoal or *leña* they used for cooking and ironing. My paternal grandfather's first wife died this way. Dad says a spark from a coal iron flew on her cotton skirt, which caught fire. She ran like a headless chicken from her thatched *bohio*, her body ablaze like a sky full of Fourth of July firecrackers, yelling *socorro, socorro,* help me, to high heaven. A campesino hoeing corn heard her screams, ran to her, and doused the flames with a donkey blanket. It was too late. When she died a few days later, she was barely twenty.

Matilde spared her daughters from most onerous chores except helping her wash and hang laundry.

Instead, they were taught to stitch and embroidery, lady-like activities expected of upper-class *señoritas*, in case a Herrera daughter was lucky enough to snag a wealthy politician or land baron with a manor house in swanky Vedado.

Matilde could be willful and manipulative.

When my mother and her sisters entered puberty, their mother suggested they cut off their long locks. She was tired of washing, combing, and brushing tangles from their silky tresses.

"Why don't you try one of those short newfangled hairstyles in the fashion magazines that you and your sisters are so fond of," Matilda said to my mom one day.

"No way," Mom protested. "I like my long hair."

As a marriageable young woman, she knew the young men from the town thought long wavy hair was a sign of purity and beauty.

Not long after, Mom's uncle Ramon and his wife, who lived in Havana, showed up at her parents' door unannounced. The childless couple doted on their unsophisticated nieces and often visited with bags full of fruit-shaped marzipan, chocolate bonbons, and a jug of Spanish olive oil for Matilde. Mom was delighted when they invited her to return with them to Havana for a short visit.

The day before Mom returned home, the couple took her on what they said was a shopping trip. She became suspicious when they led her down a narrow winding street in Old Havana and shoved her into a beauty parlor. The beautician plopped her in a chair, cut her beloved tresses to just below her ears, applied a permanent that smelled dreadful, burned her hair, and made her look like an aluminum scouring pad.

She cried all night and on the way home the next day. When my grandmother saw her daughter's shorn head, she said, " You'll be much cooler this summer."

Mom ran to her bedroom, slammed shut the door, and refused to eat for three days. She let her hair grow out to spite her mother until it reached her waist. She didn't cut it again until years later when she landed in the U.S.; short, permed hair was all the rage.

My reserved grandmother seems to have been no help to her daughters regarding sex and marriage. As a young bride, whenever Mom confided her marital troubles to her mother, Matilde's harsh response was, "Con *la cuchara que escogiste tienes que comer,* you chose your spoon, now eat with it."

She was probably thinking of her restrictive, unhappy marriage and remembered her mother saying the same.

When Matilde served dinner, she never sat with the rest of the family at the table but stood in the kitchen doorway in case her husband called for another glass of water or more bread. She ate, standing up, hunched over a small plate of food clasped in one hand, and picked at the grains of rice like a sparrow. She preferred the tail end of a loaf of bread—*el culito de pan,* she called it—and the burnt crud at the bottom of the rice pot. She was fastidious about cleanliness and spied on her husband through the half-closed bedroom door to ensure he scrubbed his privates with soap in the *palangana* of water she'd heated and left on a chair in the bedroom. She knew he sometimes tried to fool her by slipping into clean clothes.

"We may be dirt poor," she said, "but we are clean."

I recall her leaning over her *estufa de carbon* in a cotton apron, gray from too much washing, dipping a large wood spoon in a pot of steaming frijoles and blowing on it before shoving it into her mouth. Needs more salt, a touch more of oregano, or a pinch of *comino*, she would mutter. I coveted her *batidos de guayaba* and mango, the mashed fruit flesh blended with *leche condensada*, condensed milk, and a touch of vanilla. She rarely touched or kissed me or anyone else that I recall, unlike Abuelo, who stroked my hair and cradled me in his lap.

Although Mom adored— venerated—her father and always did as he said, she challenged him over the gray swallows, yellow-crested *tomeguines*, and black-as-night *toti* he kept in a cage on the front porch. She cried each time she fed them seeds or water.

"Papa, they are wild creatures; they don't belong in cages," she would implore.

One day when she went out to feed them, her father stood beside the empty birdcage.

"Olguita, you don't have to cry anymore," he said. "I let them go."

Although Abuelo doted on my teenage Mom—at times giving in to her whims for an afternoon at the town movie theater watching a Cantinflas or Maria Felix movie in the company of her married sister or mother— he quashed most of her desires.

He refused her request to play in the school band, apprentice to a cobbler, recite poems at verbenas, or attend the University of Havana, more than an hour away by bus.

"No daughter of mine is going to ride a jam-packed bus full of lecherous boys," he thundered. "Quién sabe, who knows what might happen."

A devastating *desengaño* was when he refused to let her accept an invitation from his wife's sister, Carmen, to join her in Tampa. Aunt Carmen had arranged a job for her young niece at the cigar factory across the street from her boarding house.

"NO, NO, y NO," he thundered at my fifteen-year-old mother so the neighbors next door and across the street would hear him.

"Eres una niña con mocos; you're just a snot-nosed girl," he said.

"Quién sabe what might happen."

Given my grandfather's authoritarian personality, I wasn't surprised when Mom told me that Dad was not her first choice for a husband. Her first love was Orlando, the only son of Spanish-born parents who owned a local grocery store.

Fair-skinned with light eyes, Orlando hoped to inherit his parents' store one day. Abuelo initially approved of the match. Orlando, who liked woodworking, began to build a marriage bed.

The couple waited to marry until they could save money to buy a house.

Their courtship lasted a year, and at the end of each week, he turned over his sweat-stained *pesos* and *reales* to my mother, who stored them in a locked cedar box on the top shelf of the chiffarobe in her bedroom. In return, she gave him a lock of her golden hair and a colorized portrait— she later brought it to the U.S.— taken at a photography studio.

All signs pointed to a spring wedding in the Catholic Church and a beach honeymoon in Varadero, an exclusive beach resort for wealthy Cubans and tourists back then and still today.

One afternoon a stranger carrying a bundle knocked on the front door of my grandparent's house. The woman was dressed in black, a sign of mourning.

Mom and her sisters had seen the disheveled-looking woman a few days before she showed up at the house, strolling up and down their street as if searching for something.

Mom recalls several unusual occurrences in the days before the stranger appeared. Abuela burned a pot of rice and had to toss it to the chickens. A mirror popped off the wall and shattered as her sister Carmen applied lipstick. At sunset, a toti bird flew into the living room, circled a few times, and smashed its head against a wall.

"How strange," Abuela muttered, crossing herself as she scooped up the tangle of feathers from the floor.

Abuela answered the woman's knock the following day. A threadbare shawl draped her thin shoulders, and she pressed a bundle to her chest. Her eyes were red and swollen.

"What do you want?" Matilde said sharply, using the personal "tu" pronoun to convey her elevated social status.

"I need to speak to your husband," she said, her voice barely a whisper.

"Espera aquí," Matilde ordered and slammed the door.

She rushed to the bedroom where her husband was taking his daily siesta.

"Some woman says she wants to see you."

"What does she want?"

"I don't know," Matilde muttered, but "aquí hay gallo tapao." The cockfighting expression means something underhanded is going on.

Abuelo opened the front door and invited the stranger inside. He ordered his daughters, who were embroidering pillowcases in the living room, to wait outside on the porch.

"Matilde," he ordered. "Bring two glasses of water.

The daughters pressed their ears against the closed door, straining to hear what was happening inside. They heard soft crying and whispering.

The woman emerged forty minutes later, tears staining her fatigued face. She leaped off the porch like a startled cat and disappeared down the dirt road.

Abuelo called Mom inside, shut the door, and cleared his throat.

"I have something to tell you," he said, his voice ominous.

"What?" asked Olga, alarmed.

"The woman says she has had *relaciones* with your *novio*."

"What sort of relations?"

Simon stared at the floor, took a long draw from the half-smoked cigar between his teeth, and coughed lightly.

"The child is Orlando's," he said.

"She's lying," Olga gasped.

"Whether you believe her or not is beside the point," Abuelo said, coughed again, pulled a crisp white handkerchief from his shirt pocket, and handed it to my mother.

"What is important is what you do now."

"What should I do?" said Olga, her voice faltering, her eyes misty.

"The child will always be a stone in your marriage."

"But what if it was just a fling, and he promises me never to see her again," she argued.

"I can only say what I would do if I were in your shoes."

"What would you do?"

"End it!"

Olga locked herself in her room and refused to eat or drink even her mother's herbal tea for nerves. When her sisters tiptoed past her closed door, they heard agonizing *sobs* that seeped beneath crevices of the bedroom door, permeated the corners of the rickety house, and clung to the colorless walls like Florida moss dripping from oak trees. An unearthly pain seemed to cover everything inside the house like a shroud—the rocking chairs, the mirrors, the dining table, grandfather's RCA radio, and Abuela's *estufa de carbon*-as if all their material objects had lost their usefulness and comfort. At the dinner tables, the few words they uttered lacked sparkle, and only utilitarian phrases came from their lips—hand me the salt, pass me more *plátanos*—as if everyone was mourning the death of a relative.

Weeks passed, and Mom eventually rose from her bed, splashed cold water on her face, and asked her mother for *café con leche* and *pan con mantequilla*. She nibbled on her buttered toast for a while. Then stood up, marched to the bedroom, dragged a chair over to her wardrobe, climbed up, and dug the heavy cedar box filled with money from the top shelf.

She slipped out the front door, the box tucked under her arm. Determined as an army squad headed for battle, she arrived at the front door of a handsome house near the town plaza, where she and her sisters liked to stroll Sunday afternoons and sneak peeks at boys.

The maid answered her knock.

"I want to speak to Orlando's sister," Olga said, her voice quivering.

"Take this to your brother," said Olga, shoving the box into the arms of the startled girl when she appeared at the door.

"Ask him to return my lock of hair and photograph."

She spun around and marched home.

Orlando sent Mom several letters. She returned them unopened. He sent his sister, who had light green eyes like his, to explain that the affair had been a youthful folly. He promised never to see the woman again. He begged Mom to see him.

Instead, Mom insisted he return her lock of hair and portrait, which he did a few months later when it was clear their courtship was over.

* * *

Dark-haired aunt Carmen, the youngest, most stubborn, and headstrong of my four aunts, was the family black sheep. Abuelo almost killed her and her lover one time.

Puzzled by this aunt's rash decision as a teenager to run away with a Black man who was also a babalao high priest, I asked another aunt, Caridad, why her sister had done this.

This Tia sighed, paused briefly, and said: "*se encaprichó,*" meaning her sister had become obsessed with the much older man whose skin color was a deep purple. The man and his mother were Santeria practitioners—strictly taboo for my Catholic family.

One night my hot-headed grandfather awoke to a loud noise from outside. He grabbed his policeman's revolver from the nightstand, ran to the yard, and caught the love birds smooching beneath the plantain trees.

"Coño, *carajo*, get the hell out, or I will shoot," Abuelo yelled as the terrified man zipped up his pants, turned, and fled.

Grandfather turned his gun on Carmen, who had dropped to her knees and sobbed. As he was about to shoot her, my mother and sister Caridad ran up behind him, pulled on their father's arm, and begged him not to kill their beloved sister.

Abuelo lowered his weapon and called his wayward daughter every curse word he knew—including the worst, *puta*, whore.

"I forbid you to see that *desgraciado hijo de puta* again," he bellowed. "If I catch him here again, I'll kill you both."

He grabbed Carmen by the hair, dragged her to a bedroom, locked the door, and ordered her to remain inside for 40 days—which he considered a fitting punishment.

As dawn broke on the day her confinement ended, Carmen grabbed her few clothes, wrapped them and an extra pair of shoes inside a bed sheet, jumped out the bedroom window, and went to live with her boyfriend.

Abuelo forbade his wife and remaining daughters from speaking to or visiting their disgraced sister—although they sometimes did so secretly.

"Está muerta, she's dead to us," the old man proclaimed.

After Carmen left home, her life took a dark turn. After her two young children died from unexplained causes, she left the babalao, went to Havana, and was rumored to be living in a whorehouse. Later, she married another man and had a daughter with him, but the husband left for Miami. She was almost 80 when she died in a nursing home after returning to Guira.

My aunt Zoraida's life was the most ill-fated of the four siblings. She fell in love with a young soldier of mixed race whose mother was black as a toti bird. After Abuelo nixed the match, he hand-picked her future husband—Antolin, who was born in Spain, served in the Batista army and was a family friend who often visited to play dominos, drink coffee and talk politics.

A stiff, humorless man, the bridegroom was at least 20 years older than Zoraida.

Whenever he visited, my aunt turned up her nose and ignored him. Soon, he called on her several times a week, making goo-goo eyes at Zoraida when she served him a thimbleful of coffee.

He addressed her as *mi estimada señorita Zoraida* removed his army cap, bowed, and inquired about her health. When he got up to leave, he offered her his outstretched hand, nodded, and winked as he said *buenas noches*, good night.

Disgusted by his presence, she slammed the door behind him.

"Good riddance," she muttered and went to bed.

One day her father suggested she consider marrying his good friend Antolin.

"He has a soldier's salary and will be a good provider. You and your children will never go hungry."

"No lo quiero," she said. I don't love him.

"You are almost 25," her father insisted.

"There are no suitors in sight. In time, you will learn to love him."

After her church wedding, as she tearfully packed for the train ride to a three-day honeymoon in the Pinar del Rio countryside, she confided to her sisters:

"I hope the train crashes and kills us instantly."

"Don't say that," cried my mother.

"With time, you will learn to love him," assured Caridad.

After the return to Guira, the young bride refused to join her husband at his military post.

"Take me home to my parents," she insisted.

"An army barracks is no place for a woman."

Zoraida dreaded her husband's infrequent conjugal visits to Guira and resisted when he shoved her into a bedroom and locked the door behind them. Two children, a son and a daughter, are said to have been engendered this way.

My poor aunt suffered throughout her life from neurasthenia—an old-fashioned term used to explain her outbursts of anger, steely silence that lasted for days, and other signs of emotional trauma. She sometimes directed her rage at her son, who resembled his father. When she was in a dark mood, she refused to leave her bedroom or the house and refused to eat or drink.

"Tiene el moño virado," my mother would say to warn me away from Zoraida whenever she had one of her spells. The English equivalent of the Spanish expression is, she has a bee in her bonnet.

Despite her *nervios*, when her spirits lifted, she sang while ironing, sweeping, or sewing seams. She was generous to my mother, other relatives, and neighbors.

A year after the unfortunate marriage, she gave birth to her first daughter. The girl was sickly, her legs twisted, and she couldn't walk properly until age five when a rare *jarabe, a* syrup fortified with massive doses of vitamins and minerals, is believed to have cured her.

Her son was born a year later. He was a fussy, colicky baby with light hair and blue eyes that mercilessly cried day and night and, as a child and teenager, was a menace to others and largely ignored. He liked to taunt and torture me and my sister by locking us in the outhouse in the yard.

I've heard that my aunt considered divorce but for an unusual event.

Antolin swaggered into the kitchen one afternoon wearing his soldier's uniform, gun strapped to his waist, as my aunt tried to force a tablespoon of medicine down their daughter's throat.

"Que carajo es esto," he said. "What the hell is going on here?"

The girl squirmed, spit, screamed, and shook her head as if possessed by a demonio as my grandmother helped my aunt restrain the girl to a chair. Red streaks ran down her neck and chest; some had splashed the floor.

"No quiero," moaned the girl. "Leave me alone."

"Let her go," bellowed Antolín, his right hand resting on the Colt .45 revolver on his waist.

"You heard me. Let her go," he boomed, drew his gun, and pointed it at my terrified aunt and grandmother, who froze as if they'd seen an ancestor walk out of their grave.

"Let her go, or I'll shoot *you* and then *you*," he thundered, pointing the cocked gun at the terrified women.

As my ashen-faced aunt and grandmother let go of the girl and retreated, he hoisted the hysterical child onto his shoulder and carried her to the military barracks.

Zoraida marched to her husband's garrison the following day and demanded to speak to the superior officer. The man listened to her horrific story and immediately returned the girl to her mother. Antolín was later transferred to another army post in a remote town and ordered to stay away from his family.

He was a loyal provider, however, and sent a chunk of his monthly pay to his estranged wife, and when he died years later, she received his widow's benefits.

I get chilly silence when I ask my relatives what happened to Antolin.

I never saw a photograph of him alone, with his bride or children. If pictures ever existed, I'm confident termites ate them along with my teenage Dad's handwritten décimas to my mother.

When my sister and I were young girls, and Zoraida's son was four or five years older, the boy enjoyed scaring and hurting us. After he locked me and my sister in the outhouse, he fled, laughing, to avoid a thrashing from his mother. I remember my aunt running after him waving a broom made of corn husks and yelling, "Maldito, wait till I get you!"

I liked to play alone in my grandparents' yard—a favorite game was to pluck marigold petals and use them to create faces and objects in the dirt. As I crouched under the flower bushes, absorbed in making a fairy carriage or the face of a cat with whiskers, this cousin crept up behind me and pushed with so much force that I fell to the ground, my face hitting the red dirt. My precious creations were erased. I ran crying to tell my mother, but he had already scampered away.

Mom told me he once did something similar to her. As she washed the concrete floor with a flannel rag and a *trapeador*, a T-shaped wood mop still used by Cubans today, her nephew materialized, a smirk on his pixie-shaped face.

"Take this, you bitch," he yelled and threw clods of red dirt on the floor near her feet.

"Now you have to rewash the damn floor," he giggled, turned on his heels, and dashed off to *Dios* knows where.

Once, he threw a jar of buttons at my sister so hard he busted her upper lip, and she needed three stitches. He'd caught her playing with some of the buttons he'd pilfered. He laughed when he saw the blood sprouting from her lip like one of my grandmother's red roses.

"She looks funny," he chortled and fled.

My aunt tried to protect us from her son's mischief and would yell for him to stop if she caught him pulling our hair or hitting us in the stomach.

But he'd grin and hot-tail it.

"When I catch you, you're going to get a good beating," Tia yelled after him.

He usually stayed away until his mother's temper quelled and she had gone out shopping for food or doing errands.

"Probrecito," Abuela muttered to the filthy, famished boy who reeked of rum.

She fed him some *mondongo*, heated some water, and made him wash up before his mother returned.

To this day, if I detect alcohol on someone's breath, I remember him. I have read that a particular sound, smell, or taste can trigger a traumatic memory. Was he the one who abused me that long ago night, the day Abuelo died?

I consider myself a forgiving person, but when I learned he had died—in excruciating pain lying on a dirty cot, his stomach swollen like a beached whale from alcohol poisoning—I felt relief. He can no longer hurt me or anyone else.

* * *

"Do you think Orlando came to the *unai-des-stay?*" Mom asked me a few years ago after she had recounted the story of her ill-fated romance with the grocer's son, this time within earshot of my dad in the next room.

Despite her decades in America, Mom has limited English and a strong accent leading to unusual pronunciations of English words and expressions. She calls Walmart Why Mart. She likes to use the phrase, "This is a freeee cun treee," when someone asks her to do something she would prefer not to do.

"I wonder if he's still alive," Mom sighed.

I promise to do a Google search for her former beloved, rumored to have immigrated to the U.S. I don't follow up because I wouldn't want to raise false hopes. But I sometimes imagine what Mom's life might have been like had she married well-to-do Orlando instead of my poor-as-a-church-mouse guajiro father. Would she have remained in Cuba? Would she have been happier?

* * *

My grandfather had good traits as well as bad ones. Although he opposed mixed marriages, he often invited white and Black friends to his dinner table. He tried to be fair and believed in social justice. Abuelo also had an uncanny instinct about politics on the island. He was an avid reader of El Diario de La Marina and other newspapers and listened around the clock to news on the radio. He followed the shenanigans of the political parties, the workers union, and the university students' organization. He listened to Batista's speeches, news of military and police operations, the latest strikes, economic instability, and attempts at sabotage and assassination. He tuned in one afternoon to a live report of a petty politician's takeover of Radio Reloj, his favorite station. The man announced that rebels had captured the presidential palace and killed Batista.

Batista had fled through a secret elevator behind his office. Soldiers shot the terrorists—students and young men in their 20s. They also broke down the door to the radio recording booth and fired a bullet into the head of the man who had made the premature announcement.

Mom boasts that her father was somewhat of a soothsayer for predicting that Cuba's future would be Communist.

I forgive my grandfather's misogyny and other sins. I was shocked when my mother told me he had a child out of wedlock, that no one but she knew about.

Abuelo was a product of old-world manners, and I loved him.

I remember him like this:

He rocks me on his lap as we hear a man's booming jackhammer voice on the radio. He coughs and spits into a small bowl next to him. His left arm is wrapped around my shoulder and chest in a lover's embrace. His large, age-spotted hand rests on my thigh, and I feel comforting warmth. A puro is wedged between his right thumb and index finger. He takes a puff, then another. He coughs.

I follow the smoke rings with my eyes as they float in large, small, and medium-sized circles toward the ceiling. The curls expand and evaporate as they rise. Each is a different shape—a witch, a dragon, a flower. The room fills with a sweet woodsy aroma. I bury my nose in the folds of his starched guayabera and smell caramel. He coughs again. His chest rattles.

Abuela emerges from the kitchen.

"Want some coffee, Simon?" she asks.

"Yes," he shouts above the din from the radio.

Un buchito, just a little.

She returns with a miniature white teacup filled with a syrupy black liquid. It smells like a cherry lollipop.

"Don't you dare give her any," Abuela warns, her voice trailing off as she retreats to her kitchen.

Abuelo takes the cup in his palm and sits up in his chair. He leans forward, brings the cup to his thick lips, blows on the rising steam, and takes a sip.

He runs his tongue along the rim, sighs, and leans back. He glances toward the kitchen. Abuela is out of range.

"Aquí linda," he says and winks.

"Here's your little bit of coffee."

I blow on it as he did and take a swallow. My tongue feels grainy from the grinds at the cup's bottom. I lick my lips to catch the remaining bit of sweetness. I smile, and Abuelo smiles back.

"Rico, mijita?" he says, and I nod.

"Our secret."

CHAPTER 5

FIRE!
CANDELA, MUCHACHOS

Havana, March 2004

My butt cheeks sting against the cold tile floor of a 50's era hotel bathroom in downtown Havana. I sprawl next to the toilet bowl and lean over a one-inch-thick pile of computer printouts I must destroy. They contain news stories from the U.S. about Cuba's crackdown on dissident journalists, people I hope to interview on this trip with my mother. Now, as in times past, Mom and *familia* serve as covers for my surreptitious journalistic work on the island—interviews for stories that may or may not be published, depending on the heat level of binational tensions and genuine concern about endangering my relatives.

Mom sleeps on the twin bed in the next room as I crouch in front of the old toilet, with a tank near the ceiling and a pull chain. I worry the commode might clog and overflow if I toss in too many scraps. But I have devised a strategy: scoop up a few sheets of heavy paper, tear them into bite-size strips, drop them into the toilet bowl, and gently pull the chain. I count to 100 in my head, wait for the bowl to clear, and repeat.

What if the guests next door and above and below me complain about the gurgling from constant flushing? I'll say it's from a bad case of diarrhea.

When we checked into the once elegant, now decrepit 40s-era hotel across from the University of Havana, my well-honed paranoia about Communist Cuba kicked in. I hear strange clicks and buzzing when I pick up the hotel room telephone. Who's listening?

Last night a journalist for the state-run news agency appeared as Mom and I finished our after-meal *cafecitos. I* was about to take a taxi to an apartment in Old Havana to interview dissidents.

"*Que pasa?*" Raul asked cheerfully as I glanced up from my coffee cup and saw him standing awkwardly behind the empty chair by our table.

"*Todo bien?*" Is everything OK?

"Porque preguntas, why do you ask?"

"Can I sit?" he says, more a statement than a question. Before I can respond, he jerks back the chair from the table and sits beside us.

I peek at my wristwatch and tap the tile floor with the toe of my high heel shoe. The interview subjects expect me in less than an hour.

Raul reaches inside a crumpled paper bag in his lap. He pulls out two copies of Bohemia, the pre-revolutionary news magazine famous in the '50s for its graphic black-and-white photos of dead bodies—teenagers and men mutilated and murdered by Batista's henchmen.

He splays the tabloids on the table like a painted fan, leans toward me, and taps the newsprint with an index finger.

"For you and your mother," he grins and settles back in his chair.

I thank him, and he speaks in rapid-pace, run-on Spanish for 20 minutes or so, leaving little to no opening for me or my mom to talk.

I glance at my watch again—quarter to nine. Mom excuses herself; she is going to bed.

"I have to go too," I insist, but Raul resumes his monologue. I don't want him to become suspicious or think I'm rude by standing up and marching away.

I place my elbows on the table, sweaty palms beneath my chin, and look directly into his caramel-colored eyes.

The bugged phone, the unannounced late-night intrusion by this man who acts as if he were my friend. He knows what I am planning. A voice nudges me to go ahead and tell him what I plan to do later that evening.

"If I were to speak to some dissident journalists," I ask, my voice quivering, "will I get into trouble?"

His thin lips turn ghost white against his milk chocolate complexion as he scans the nearly empty dining room as if searching for something.

"Of course not," he mutters, squirms in his chair, and fixes his vision on a broken lamppost outside the window behind me. After we exchange a few more pleasantries, he coughs, smiles, and waves good night.

I race to my third-floor hotel room, call the journalists I plan to meet, and reschedule our interview for the following day.

"Something's come up," I say, taking ragged breaths.

"I can't explain now. We can chat in the lobby tomorrow if you come to my hotel."

I hang up, collapse on the thin, lumpy mattress, close my eyes, take several deep breaths to slow my racing heart, and try to think of the ocean waves nearby. Mom is asleep in her bed, in her usual position—on her right side, hands beneath her cheek to prevent her stiff blonde bouffant from being mussed.

My clattering brain suddenly remembers what I've hidden in the closet—reams of U.S. newsprint packed inside my Samsonite suitcase. I feel panic. Exiles have been imprisoned for smuggling illicit, subversive literature and anti-Cuba propaganda into the island. I panic. What if they discover the news stories hidden in the closet, making me the subject of tomorrow's screaming front-page headline—"Contraband Found, Miami Journalist Detained."

I spring from the bed, rush toward the closed closet doors, pull out the wad of computer paper, and get to work in the bathroom.

* * *

A young high school teacher I interviewed once wrote me a letter after being fired from his job and hounded by Communist authorities because of our conversation in the living room of my family's home.

"There are spies even in our own house," he wrote in the letter and attributed the quote to the diary of Anne Frank, a young Jewish girl killed by the Nazis. I searched her diary for the saying but could not find it. No matter. I understood his meaning.

I won't use his name because I promised not to. I will call him Maestro. He taught history at the high school in my hometown, and we met in the '80s on an early return trip. The hour-long conversation set off a chain of betrayals by family members and others.

One incident occurred a few years after he and I met, and I still reported for the Miami Herald about political intrigue and criminal shenanigans in Little Havana. It involved a mysterious photograph of me and a man in Cuba that someone had turned over to the Florida Department of Law Enforcement. Over lunch, a news source, a federal prosecutor remarked that the photograph shows me "in a compromising position" with a high-level Communist agent. Did I know who the man was? He asked.

"I have no idea," I protested, then remembered when I danced at Tropicana Nightclub with someone who said he was a tourism official. I remember we had a few beers. After the show, he invited me to the dance floor and stepped on the toes of my pointed heels, causing me to lose my balance.

"I think I know," I finally said, describing the tortured dance at the cabaret with the fellow I thought was a tour operator.

"Well, he was a spy," the prosecutor said.

"A top operative with the Cuban security forces."

"They snapped your picture."

"To what end?"

"To discredit your journalism."

"Oh," I said and chuckled.

"Lesson learned," I said.

"Never trust a Cuban man who can't dance to a proper son."

* * *

A cousin from Guira set up the interview with Maestro.

"I have a friend who has asked to meet you," he said, with a crooked grin, his beady eyes squinting.

"He wants to speak to you because you are a reporter."

I don't remember much of our conversation, only that we sat facing each other on rattan rockers in my family's dark living room. It was summertime, and the tropical heat was so oppressive that breathing was hard. Oddly, someone shut the front door and closed the shutters to block our view from passersby. The cousin who introduced us, who was in his mid-20s, sat somewhere behind us, hidden in shadows in a corner. His mother, my aunt, fussed about in the kitchen, probably preparing the evening meal.

When Maestro knocked and we opened the door, he carried a battered leather briefcase. He was short, stocky, in his 30's, with a gentle smile, soft palms, and a forthright manner. Serious. As we sat down, he explained that he had graduated from the University of Havana with a degree in history and intended to return for more study.

I listened quietly to his complaints about the Communist education system. He was only allowed to teach history from a Marxist-Leninist perspective—not a word about the U.S. or world history. His government-mandated textbook was used to indoctrinate students in Communist ideology. He was no longer allowed to refer to his pupils as "students" but as *pioneros*, young pioneers. He said students were being tricked into believing that God didn't exist.

A Communist party official's recent visit to his classroom had greatly disturbed him. The *miliciano* wore olive-green fatigues and asked his permission to speak to the class.

He ordered the children to shut their eyes from his perch at the front of the classroom.

"Now pray to God for candy," he said.

The children did as they were told. Nothing was on their desktops when he asked them to open their eyes.

"Now, close your eyes and ask Fidel for candy," he prompted.

An excited murmur arose from the classroom, and the children again shut their eyes. When they opened them, a pile of candy had magically appeared on top of their desks.

"*Acuerdanse*, remember," he barked.

"This is what the revolution does for you!"

Maestro is angered by certain government dictates. Young children are denied milk after turning two, and 12, 13, and 14-year-olds are sent to coed government camps in summer to harvest sugarcane. All for the sake of the revolution.

He spoke so fast that I had difficulty taking down his quotes in my skinny reporter's notebook and had to ask him to repeat what he'd said a few times. I regret losing that notebook, and over the years, I've searched attics and basements for it to prove to myself that the interview occurred.

We chatted for over an hour that day—with a break for an espresso served by my silent, stone-faced aunt. When he rose to leave, he gave me a forceful handshake.

"Thank you for listening."

When I returned to Miami, I forgot about the interview. I doubted I could corroborate what he had told me. If I published the story, Miami's right-wing idealogues would consider me a friend and hero; the Cuban government, *un espia*—a spy—forbidden to ever return to my country.

I published an article based on that 1980 trip with my parents about the left-wing government's agrarian reform program. It contrasted two campesino families—one that supported the revolution and received free seed and fertilizer; and another family who opposed the new regime, did not receive government subsidies, and struggled to grow enough food to eat. They considered leaving for the U.S.

My story was factual and balanced. So I thought.

Right-wing exiles denounced it on the Miami airwaves calling the story Cuban government propaganda.

"That Herald reporter—Zita Arocha—is a Comunista," crowed the best-known exile radio host in Miami at the time, with a strong emphasis on the word Communist. My parents, avid followers of the news out of Miami, heard the broadcast in Tampa. They called immediately to say they were worried.

* * *

Cuba, 1986

Mom and I sit in the kitchen as my tia Zoraida pours us coffee when a young woman I don't recognize walks in and introduces herself. She is the granddaughter of the neighbors across the street. Her family and my family have been intimate and friendly for decades, sharing holidays, birthdays, births, weddings, and deaths.

"My grandmother has something for you," says the young woman. I notice she is shivering despite the heat.

She grabs my elbow and leads me to a house much like that of my relatives across the dusty street.

When I walk inside, she introduces me to a woman of about 70 who seems vaguely familiar. I must have known her as a child. Her skin is chocolate-colored, and her kinky short white curls remind me of the seafoam created by churning waves.

She motions for me to sit on a twin bed in a corner. I obey, cross my legs, and lean back awkwardly, my hands resting on the edges of the faded brown mattress cover.

She disappears behind a doorway covered by a yellow curtain and emerges a few minutes later, clutching a sealed envelope. I notice that my name is scrawled in large script across its face.

"Léalo read it," she orders.

"It's from someone I love like a son."

The thin yellow paper reminds me of onion skin, and the pages crackle as I unfold them. It is a letter, six pages long, covered in blue cursive, front and back, with words flowing into the margins.

"Estimada Zita," it begins. "I hope this letter finds you and your loved ones in good health and spirits."

I realize the letter is from the Maestro. He writes to explain what occurred to him after our meeting five years before.

He wrote that when he returned to school a week after our interview, two State Security agents waited for him and blocked his entry to the classroom. Instead, the men forced him into an isolated room inside the schoolhouse. After they asked him to sit, they repeated word for word his conversation with the *periodista,* a journalist from Miami.

His comments to the reporter were "counter-revolutionary," *a crime.* After the three-hour closed-door interrogation, they ordered him to leave and never return.

Later, he said, local party members held an official hearing, forcing him to sign a document admitting errors in his thinking and crimes against the state. His punishment: permanent expulsion. He would never teach again.

I glance up and blink away tears. I search the glum face of the older woman, but she is silent, expressionless, inscrutable. She does not return my gaze. I am being judged, I realize, and I feel nauseous.

I return to the letter: After his expulsion, he went to the U.S. Interests Section in Havana and begged for permission to emigrate. He explained in detail what had happened. The consular officials said they couldn't help because he hadn't been imprisoned.

Later, he was assigned a job tending pigs on a government farm—the only work suitable for traitors. He and his wife subsisted on his meager wages and donations of money and food from family and friends.

I felt a sharp stab in my chest when I read the next paragraph.

"My decision to speak to you some years ago has cost me dearly... I was never sentenced, but I will never again raise my head. I am a marginalized person, a pariah...I will carry this sentence for the rest of my life."

Next came a knife twist.

"I fell into a political trap," he wrote. "But you shouldn't feel responsible for what happened. When bad things are destined to happen, they happen. Nothing would have happened if I had gone home after school that day."

I wiped away a tear and heard a voice in my head: *or I had not agreed to interview you.*

He ended the letter asking for my help to leave. Don't publish or write anything more about me, he noted.

"It will only make matters worse."

I trembled as I folded the curling pages and returned them to their creased envelope. I must have appeared dazed because the older woman offered me water. I asked for his address in Havana as she handed me the glass.

* * *

A few days later, I met Maestro at a non-descript bar-café in a decaying Havana neighborhood near where he lived. We had a few beers and talked. I tripped and fell on broken tiles on my way to the bar. My knees were scraped and bruised. When Maestro saw my wounds, he wet his handkerchief with water and wiped away the blood. Later, he repeated the pathetic story from the letter. When we parted three hours later, I pressed three $20 bills into his palm and promised to help.

After returning home to Washington, D.C., I went to speak with a Cuban American Congresswoman from Miami. I thought she would offer help. Instead, after hearing his story, she rolled her heavily made-up eyes a few times and said she was sorry. Still, the U.S. government was only interested in helping political prisoners. There were plenty of them already waiting in line for an entry permit. Maestro didn't qualify.

"Thanks," I muttered and scurried out the thick wood doors of her Capitol Hill office.

On my way to the Metro train, I felt relieved. I had kept my promise to Maestro; I'd done all I could. I didn't hear from him again for the next ten years.

* * *

Journalists live and die by the creed to not harm, which is also a primary tenet of most religions. What if you cause harm unintentionally? Who is at fault? How do you make amends? There is no simple answer. No doubt, someone, a family member, overheard our long-ago conversation and reported it. That person betrayed me and destroyed the teacher's life. This knowledge doesn't absolve me or mitigate the unwitting role I played in Maestro's downfall. Or the guilt and rage I still feel over our betrayal.

The ground sways beneath me each time I visit, and my steps falter. The solid sense of who I believe I am–journalist, wife, mother, and citizen of the United States–crumbles like the stone chunks that fall from Havana's decrepit buildings on the sidewalks below.

I have tripped and fallen several times on the jagged Colonial-era cobblestones of the old city. When I was on my way to see Maestro and again on a trip with my husband, I slipped on the 15th-century pave stones of the malecón, injuring my knees.

Sometimes, Cuba swallows me like a mountain of rice, and I cry inconsolably, listening to the old boleros, rumbas, and the sones from my mother's time. Or over a simple memory—slurping ketchup from hotdogs with my Havana cousins in the back seat of their father's car after we visit the downtown zoo.

I erect defenses thick as seawalls around the old city, and alarm bells go off in my head as soon as my plane touches down. Experience has taught me: beware whom you trust.

The taxi driver takes me and my mother to our hometown and hangs around listening to family conversations. She's most likely an informant. The overly solicitous tour guide I hired over the Internet to visit Pinar Del Rio acts surprised that the Cuban government has permitted me–a U.S. journalist–into the country. With his linen guayabera, polished new shoes, and digital watch, is he a plant for the exile *derecha*, the far right? It's common knowledge that right-wing ideologues—some are terrorists with U.S backing—sneak into Cuba to gather intelligence and cause mischief.

My husband and I met a stranger outside our Vedado hotel. The man offers to show us around the city. We accept. A few days later, he asked us to give an "informal" talk to university students about public relations. Private business and industry don't exist in Cuba. What's his motive?

Another time a young, fresh-faced security guard approaches us at twilight as we stroll a downtown sidewalk to our hotel. Where are you from? He asks. When we say the U.S.-Mexico border, he names some journalists we know from El Paso and Ciudad Juarez.

How did he know? Who's watching?

There are various betrayals. To lie, obfuscate or spy for nefarious purposes are the most obvious. But there's a different type of duplicity. It involves suppressing memory and is just as destructive. To deny, conceal or distort the past seems like sacrilege and is self-betrayal, an erasure of who we were, are now, and will be tomorrow. To retain our memories—both pleasant and painful— feels good and faithful. As a journalist, I plumb the recollections of others for facts about their lives and do the same in interviews with my parents, aunts, uncles, and cousins— on both sides of the sea. I've unearthed little or nothing besides what I already know from my memories and listening to family stories. Instead of providing new revelations and answers to my questions, they reply *no se; no me recuerdo; I don't remember.*

I am shocked. My memories of Cuba at age four and six are more lucid than those of my relatives, even though they were adults when the events I ask about occurred. Their amnesia, honest or duplicitous, at first dismays me. Still, later I understand that remembrances can serve a self-protective purpose and are as porous as water pouring through a sieve.

My aunt Caridad doesn't remember our visit to the zológico, the Havana zoo, on New Year's Eve 1958, until I show her the photograph of my sister, me, and her two young children dressed in cowboy outfits sitting on a wall of the zoo. Do you remember what happened that night? I ask her. She claims to have but a vague memory of the traumatic incident. It is a colorized scene engraved in memory of my unsuspecting uncle driving us into a military fort as guards point their guns and shout, "Stop, or we'll shoot." I can still see my frightened uncle jumping from the car, hands above his head, screaming at the dark faces on the wall above: "*No disparen,* don't shoot. There are women and children in the car." The guards lowered their guns, and one came down to talk. My uncle convinced him he had taken a wrong turn into the installation on the new U.S.-financed highway under the bay on the way home to Guanabacoa.

None of the relatives there can recall details of what happened the day my grandfather died, the evening I was assaulted. After the assailant left, I sat in a rocking chair, sobbing beside my grandfather's body. My mother, asleep in another room, heard me and came.

"What happened," she asked, rubbing her groggy eyes.

"Nada," I said, hiding my face in my rumpled nightgown. Nothing.

"What happened," asked my aunt Zoraida when she approached me with a cup of calming tilo.

"Nervios," said my mother. "A bad dream."

Fifty years later, my husband and I took a taxi to Guanabacoa, where another aunt, Caridad, lived before her family left Cuba for Florida in the mid-60s.

The neighborhood was the site of the midnight explosion. I remember the night Batista fled, and the powerful blast threw my mom off the bed. I've never known what caused it, and I hope to learn more on this trip.

As we drive through the main avenue in the blazing noonday sun, I recognize the narrow lime-green structure that once housed the former Café Regil, where my uncle worked as a young married salesman.

As the taxi crawls down a bumpy side road, I spot my family's former concrete-block house, freshly painted and with a sign nailed next to the front door frame—"Block Committee for the Defense of the Revolution."

I knock, and a friendly woman in her mid 40's opens the door and greets us. "I didn't know your relatives," she says. "Would you like to come inside?"

After we sit in the living room, she explains that she lives alone. Her children, the University of Havana graduates, are accomplished professionals with their own families. I glance at the ceiling and see my aunt's cherished art deco glass chandelier, which her husband purchased decades earlier at the once fancy downtown department store that celebratory crowds burned down after Batista's fall.

Is my uncle's revolver still hidden among the pink and white petals? I do not dare ask.

As we leave the area, I recognize an elderly couple staring at us from the porch of their house across the street. I vaguely remember them. When I greet them, they ask about my aunt's and her family's health. They want to know what they do in America. After I oblige, I inquire about the decades-old explosion that had left still-visible cracks in the outside walls of the neighborhood's then-modern concrete block houses.

"What explosion?" asks the man.

"You know," I press, "the explosion the night Batista fled when we all ran outside into the street in our pajamas."

The couple stares at me blankly.

"No se," says the man.

"I don't remember," says his wife.

Perhaps they *have* forgotten or prefer not to remember.

Adios, I wave.

A few days later, we spent a day in Guira with my cousin Mirta, her son, his wife, and their three young daughters. They live in my grandparents' old house, now partitioned into several rooms. They have added an indoor commode and shower.

Later, I visit Nene and Mario, two of my father's five brothers who long ago traded their rustic *chozas* on the family farm for tiny government-provided houses in the heart of town.

They speak softly into my Sony recorder and offer brief greetings to my parents in Florida.

During this trip, my once romantic perception of home shifted again when I learned that a cousin's husband left on a raft and drowned in the ocean on the way to Florida. She is raising their nine-year-old son. Another female cousin whispers in my ear. "Will you help my son if he appears outside your door one day?"

Count on me, I say.

When I visit the home of a male cousin, a group of shirtless young men huddles in the corner of the backyard near the chicken coops. They are whispering. Later, I learn they are plotting to leave the island shortly.

These revelations—a young father's death at sea and the secret risky plans of others to risk their lives to flee—challenge my recollection of a lush, languid, magical island home. My memory of Cuba is a mirage. She produces not just sugar, tobacco, rum, and sultry rhythms but bodies in motion, bodies in flight, bodies thrust into the ocean on makeshift rafts and inner tubes, and bodies that die at sea for what? Cuba is a cruel lover. I'm not sure I want her anymore.

As my disillusionment grows—will I ever *want* to return here?—so does an urgent need to resurrect submerged memories. I spend two hours sitting across from Cousin Mirta at the kitchen table with my tape recorder.

When and where were my grandparents born?

No sé.

What were the names of their parents?

She shakes her head.

When did Aunt Carmen meet her barber husband and move to Tampa?

No se.

What were the names of my aunt's two babies who died?

No me recuerdo.

How did they die? Where are they buried?

She sighs and twirls the thin gold ring on her index finger. The ring is missing its stone.

Her face brightens. She remembers something: The ring was a gift to her mother from Aunt Carmen on one of her long-ago summer visits to Cuba. She mentioned that its ruby was lost before her mother died. "I hope to replace the stone one day," Mirta confides.

As a girl of thirteen, this now wrinkled gray-haired septuagenarian woman taught me to play with marbles and walked me several blocks to the Catholic nursery school daily.

My throat constricts, and my lungs feel like they are squeezed like sea sponges. I am light-headed and exhausted, as if I've climbed a mountain without stopping to catch my breath. I feel bereft but am not sure why.

Later, I think I know. Although I left at age four, I remember more about Cuba's pre-revolutionary past than my relatives who remained. I alone am intent on recollecting what happened.

A few days later, my husband and I finagle a visit to the newspaper archives of a cultural institute in Havana. It is our second visit to the place. As we walked into the building for the first time, workers showed up to fumigate for mosquitos carrying dengue. The librarian politely asked us to leave.

A friend arranges a second visit on a Saturday, the day before our departure. The place is closed on weekends.

We doubt the librarian will show up. But she arrives at nine sharp, officiously unlocks the door, and lets us inside.

"What do you want?" she asks in a huffy tone, flipping on the weak yellow, fluorescent light to reveal a dozen rectangular, gleaming wood tables scattered in rows throughout the gloomy, cavernous room.

I am searching for facts for a *libro de memorias*, a memoir, I explain, and immediately worry that I've given her too much information. But I tell her what I am after–copies of Revolución, Diario la Marina, and Revista Bohemia newspapers. I request specific dates: April 27, 1952–my birth date– and December 31, 1958, to January 7, 1959, the first week of the takeover by the revolutionary government.

She raises an eyebrow and waves me toward a tall wooden file cabinet filled with musty index cards. I use a three-inch pencil–the only writing implement allowed inside–to write down in my notebook the Dewey decimal numbers of the issues I seek. The clock above my head ticks by the second, and I need to rush, like a miner panning for gold as the sun sets.

The library cards indicate that the newspapers are on microfiche. I hold my breath as I approach the table with a Soviet-era microfiche machine. The librarian appears by my side suddenly.

"Lo siento," she apologizes. "The lightbulb burned out five years ago; no replacements exist."

"What about the actual newspapers? Can I look at those?" I plead.

She lowers her voice. She seems embarrassed.

"We had a flood last year; there was extensive damage. The volumes are quite fragile. I'm not allowed to let you see them."

"Please," I implore. "At least allow me to see the least damaged volumes."

She hesitates. I can tell she's considering the possibility. I hold my breath and play my last card—the Queen of Diamonds.

"My husband and I want to donate to your library."

I see David giving me a dirty look from the corner of my eye.

I plunge ahead. "We really would like to help."

She walks away and disappears among the moldy stacks and emerges a few minutes later, her arms full of bound newsprint—issues of *Revolución* during the first week of 1959, issues of *Bohemia* for the same period, and a heavy tome filled with *Diarios* from my birth year.

Wow. I lick the point of my miniature pencil and get to work, scribbling down dates, headlines, the contents of ads, and descriptions of paragraphs from a few critical stories. The edges of the yellowed pages crumble in places. I touch each page with the tenderness of a mother caressing her newborn. I am acutely aware of the historical significance of these fragile broadsheets filled with photos of a young bearded triumphant Castro and revolutionary leaders Camilo Cienfuegos and Ché Guevara riding on jeeps through the provinces toward Havana.

I recognize iconic photos of rebels before triumphant crowds in the capital city's streets as they waited for the arrival of the victors; one of Castro, jubilant and beaming, with three doves perched on his shoulders, speaking to the people from the balcony of a hotel; of a guajiro wrapped around an electric pole to catch a glimpse of the new commander. Other photos show crowds smashing casino slot machines and parking meters of the politician Miguel Urrutia's return to Cuba from exile to assume the presidency of la *nueva república.* As expected, Fidel deposed him a month later and declared himself maximum *líder.*

I touch history, I realize. These fragile volumes and flimsy pages do not exist anywhere else. In their present condition, they won't last much longer. I take in the scent of library dust and glue embedded in the 60-year-old newsprint. As I flip to another page, I can't believe what I see: a story in a January 1959 edition of *Revolución* about an explosion in Guanabacoa—10,000 tons of munitions blown up by Castro sympathizers to prevent Batista's soldiers from seizing the weapons. My knees feel shaky. I didn't just imagine the explosion. Here is the proof that it happened.

I hear a burst of clicks. David is snapping pictures with his Nikon.

The librarian appears.

"No pictures," she says sharply.

"Perdón," I say.

"He promises he won't do it again." I give David another dirty look. He grins, lowers the Nikon, and tucks it into his open shirt. The librarian leaves us.

I open the volume with copies of *El Diario de la Marina,* the official government mouthpiece for the Batista regime.

I thumb the pages expectantly until I find April 27, 1952. There she is, beneath the masthead in bold print, just as my mother has told me many times—Santa Zita. The name my grandfather chose for me after reading the day's paper.

David yanks out his camera, hunches over the broadsheet, and snaps pictures. I am done.

"Gracias," I say and press two twenty-dollar bills in the librarian's palm.

The following morning, we land in Cancun, turn on the TV in our ocean-view hotel room, and learn that *el caballo, el caiman, el comandante*—names people use to refer to Fidel—has relinquished power to his brother Raul because "extreme stress" has affected his health.

* * *

Where is Maestro now? Forty years have passed since we spoke in the living room of my family's home, and he was stripped of his livelihood and dignity. Perhaps he made it to Europe or Latin America. Maybe he's in Miami. Is his wife with him? Does he have grandchildren?

He wrote me a second letter two decades after our ill-fated first encounter. Things were no better, he said. Would I send him a few hundred dollars to tide him over? Was I returning to Cuba?

I did not write or send money. I have returned to Cuba several times but have not looked him up or visited the neighbor who first handed me his letter. I'm not sure why. Cowardice? A lingering sense of impotence and guilt? Betrayal by a relative is devastating. Far easier to pretend or forget it happened. Maybe Maestro was correct to say bad things happen because they were meant to happen. I put it another way: Our combined karma brought us together that long-ago afternoon and produced unimaginable consequences. I shed *lágrimas negras* for us all.

> *"Our world is filled with exiles.*
> *How can they sing when they are so far from home?*
> *And where is home?*
> *And how do they find it again?"*
> —Margaret Guenther, *Walking Home*

EPILOGUE

Tara Mandala,
July 2021

I return to reconnect with nature, meditate and briefly escape from a global pandemic. The emerald-green San Juan Mountains inspire the finishing touches of my memoir. Also, solitude, silence, and isolation are respites from the worry of becoming sick or dying. I feel safe within this secluded shelter, closed to outsiders except for the skeletal staff and intrepid retreatants like me.

Ratna cabin is occupied, so I stay in Prajna, which means wisdom. I catch myself comparing things, *esto de eso*, this from that. I miss the plummet from Ratna's front door and the brisk downhill walk to the secret meadow. Most of all, I long for my demon tree, its stark trunk, and charred and snarled limbs. She inspired many meditations during my previous retreat.

Prajna has perks. It's located on flatter ground and is a quarter mile from the road where I parked my shiny new red Toyota van, bought after trade-in for my hybrid green Camry, which I still miss. I call it my Dakini car after female deities said to live in the Pure Land. The cabin has modern conveniences: a solar collector, a small refrigerator, a composting toilet off the front porch, and a water pump a few feet from the French double doors where I wash my dishes and hair. There is extra space for books, practice materials, and kitchen utensils. I no longer need to lug fifty-gallon jugs of water bottles and grocery sacks up and down the mountain. My bad knees appreciate the gentler landscape. The provisions I brought with me should last the week.

Stop comparing; I remind myself. The point of dharma is to abide without abode. You will find a new demon tree for your meditation.

Since my drum teacher's cremation many summers ago, my immediate relatives in Cuba and Florida have disappeared like fragile charms falling from an old bracelet. They are ghosts now and live as memories in my book.

My eighty-seven-year-old father collapsed in the hallway of Buena Vida nursing home in Tampa in 2014.

"Me muero, I'm dying," he muttered to a young nurse on her first night on the job. As she walked him to his bedroom, he floated to the terrazzo floor like the handkerchief he had kept in his breast pocket all his life.

My sister called later that night as I pulled into the driveway of my home in Las Cruces. I was planning a trip to see him in two days.

"Come home," she said. "Dad's gone."

We buried *el sinsonte de* Guira in my husband's finest navy-blue suit in a shade-covered plot in the Garden of Memories in Tampa, beneath two palm trees and a giant stone monument of a bible. He and Mom picked out the spot and paid it off on the installment plan.

Dad had hoped to outlive his nemesis, Fidel Castro. He even wrote a *décima* about Fidel. The Cuban leader lived two more years. Unlike my dad's simple graveside service, a cortege of politicians and admirers followed Fidel's body from Havana to the far east city of Santiago, where he was buried beside the grave of Cuba's national hero and liberator, Jose Marti, whom Castro revered. Throngs of grieving citizens, wringing their hands and sobbing, lined the streets of cities and country towns along the route to pay respects to their beloved comandante.

"I cried," one woman told me, "as if I'd lost my father."

Unsurprisingly, across the Florida Straits in Little Havana, Tampa, New Jersey, and other U.S. cities, thousands of exiles cheered the death of their life-long enemy and what they predicted would soon follow: the end of Communism in their homeland. From wherever he might be now, I imagine Fidel bemused and observing the celebration, thinking: "I may be gone, but rumors of Communism's death are greatly exaggerated—Hasta la Victoria Siempre! Viva la Revolución."

Mom outlived my father by almost a decade. She died last year at age ninety-four from complications from dementia. She spent her final years in an assisted living facility run by a loving and attentive Cuban couple and caretakers who spoke to her in Spanish and cooked her favored *frijoles negros*. The couple had worked in banking and education back home. One of the caregivers had been a doctor on the island.

During Mom's stay, they treated her to afternoon *cafecitos*. Because Mom had diabetes, the workers sometimes hand-fed her bites of caramel flan. Even after dementia erased most of her recollections and she could no longer speak, walk or feed herself, she perked up when my sisters and I visited. Whenever I sang her favorite song, "Guajira Guantanamera," or whispered José Martí poems into her ear, her foggy blue eyes fluttered open and shone like searchlights. A broad smile would suffuse her smooth, unwrinkled face, and she'd croak along to the tune, mouthing a word or a line until she grew tired or bored and began to nod off.

"Basta, that's enough," she ordered as if I were still ten. She said the same as a hospital nurse tried to draw blood from her shriveled finger, now purple from too much poking. She took her last breath two days later in a hospice facility.

Her sisters, Zoraida and Carmen, died on the island where they were born; Caridad, and her brother, Orlando, died in Tampa.

Dad's siblings, Mario, Corucho, el Nene, Juana, Ernestina, and Caridad, died in their hometown, still yearning for a taste of the promised land.

Only his estranged sister Hilda died in America.

Mario visited Dad in Tampa once. They spent a month reminiscing about their boyhood on the farm, reciting décimas, going to my father's evangelical church, and doing small plumbing jobs. He vowed to return to Tampa before long.

"Don't worry, mi hermano," Mario said, flashing a smile bright as a party lantern as he caught the plane home. "Nos vemos pronto, we'll see each other soon."

He was killed by a car as he crossed a street on his bike not long after returning to Cuba.

Before my dad died, he also reunited with his sister Hilda, who, as a teenager, ran away with a farmhand and was presumed dead after Dad searched for her in the red-light districts of Havana. She returned to Guira in her 60s and immigrated later to the U.S. The long-separated siblings spent a joyful day together in Miami, where Hilda lived with a daughter and son-in-law a few years before she died of cancer.

My troubled cousin also *cantó el manisero*, as my parents often said of family members and friends who had died. The phrase, still common today among exiles and on the island, is from a famous 1930s *pregón* about a peanut vendor who asks people to buy some peanuts before he's gone.

This cousin suffered from late-stage alcoholism and lingered in an ill-equipped rural clinic for weeks. There were no painkillers to treat him. My family said he was delirious and begged the doctors to kill him. If you believe in karma, his agony was the reward for his cruelty.

My uncle Humberto, the former coffee salesman who married my aunt Caridad and built a small fortune selling sirloin and *palomilla* steaks to exiles, succumbed to heart disease and a stroke in his 80s. Several exiles spoke at his memorial about how the Tampa butcher had helped pay their law and medical school tuition. His wife, Caridad, my mother's other sister, also outlived her husband and died in her 90s after a fall in the marble bathroom of their sprawling ranch house.

My friend Humberto, whom I met in El Paso and still intent on becoming a doctor despite his advanced age, overdosed on rum and pain pills during a trip to Austin with his wife to visit their only daughter's grave. The young woman, a college student, had been murdered years earlier by a besotted boyfriend. After Humberto's death, his wife invited me to lunch, and we spent several hours reminiscing about his colorful life and adventures as an exile in Spain and the U.S.

She confided that Humberto had never recovered from the double loss of his young daughter and his "beloved Cuba."

Maestro, my hometown's disgraced history teacher, may also be gone. If so, I hope his wish to leave Cuba for the U.S. or another country came true. I want to believe he has grandchildren and eventually returned to teaching.

Before I left home for another mountain retreat, my husband David urged me to finish the book.

"It's done," David said, a touch of exasperation in his gruff voice.

"Send it out."

"Yes, I know, you are right."

I've resisted arriving at the end, but I am unsure why. Is it from fear? What will my relatives think? What if I offend? What if one side or the other twists my words and distorts their meaning? My worries are valid, given my past experiences with the Cuban political right and left.

I know now that memories are imperfect, contorted, and misshapen by perception, feeling, and emotion—but they are mine, only mine. Our unique life experiences fashion our version of reality.

I've also resisted ending my book of memories from a belief—I know it is irrational—that the people from my past will remain alive as long as I write about them, just as the long-ago disturbed immigrant child thought she would not die as long as she forced herself to stay awake.

Having captured the essence of my parents, grandfather, relatives, and country in words like butterflies in a net, I'm disinclined to let them go.

Unlike deadline-driven reporting, finishing a book can take one year or ten. That's okay, or *oka*, as they say in Cuba.

Writing has been a journey to self-awareness, the forgiveness of those who wronged me, graceful acceptance of life's fragility and impermanence—and an exorcism of my exile past.

Each day I consciously choose to practice detachment—from my grandfather's corpse, my cousin's rage, and my sickle-shaped island.

Like most exiles, I have felt displaced, odd, an outsider, separated in time and space from what I believed was my authentic self—a four-year-old child in Cuba—only to realize that there is no such thing as a fixed self or a permanent home. Self is fluid. Exile is a state of mind. I'm home wherever I happen to be—in Las Cruces, Tampa, Guira, Colorado. My search for a home is finished.

Tsultrim, my dharma teacher, once asked if I considered myself Cuban or American.

"I'm a hyphenated American like most of us," I chuckled, then added with a grin, "and a guajira like my dad."

I am all those things and many more.

As a journalist, I've devoted my life to searching for answers to questions of who, what, where, when, how, and why, which is the most challenging. Often there are no definitive answers. Bad things happened—the nighttime assault, my angry young father lashing me across the legs with a belt buckle when I was a toddler, and my mother soothing the injuries in a tin of cool water; my country roiled by revolution; a decent man destroyed by ideology.

I will never know why these things happened; it no longer matters.

The book is concluded, but I have a final question.

Have I finally said goodbye to my Cuba? Will I revisit her? Will she let go of me? *No sé.* Life is fluid and unpredictable. Maybe, maybe not. It doesn't matter.

My Aunt Zoraida, who died in her bed wearing Mom's gift of U.S.-made tennis shoes, dealt with the negative experiences of her past by pretending they never happened.

On one of my trips home—I've forgotten the exact dates, and the chronology no longer matters to me—Mom had gone out to deliver gifts to some female relatives and left me alone with Zoraida and her daughter Mirta, who looks like a carbon copy of her mother. It was mid-morning in January, and we stood in the dining room drinking coffee as a soft breeze wafted inside from the backyard, where a few chickens scratched the dirt. I remember the room smelled of fresh coconut water.

"Tia, where did I sleep the night Abuelo died?"

I've never asked her, or anyone else, this question before.

On this trip home, Zoraida is in her mid-70s, her back *jorobada* like the rounded handle of a walking cane. She looks morose when I ask this question, a trick question because I know the answer. I slept in the front bedroom facing the street, her room, when her husband paid conjugal visits. When I slept there, someone attacked me. I can't recall who it was.

A good reporter, I am leading up to what I want to know. Who was it?

"Vamos afuera, let's go outside," Zoraida orders, motioning toward the backyard. I follow behind her brisk pace, and so does Mirta. We stand next to a clump of banana trees, which face a large cage on stilts where my family keeps the cat at night for safety. During severe food shortages, Cubans have been known to eat cats and dogs.

Zoraida scans the verdant landscape and gazes up at the row of tall, elegant palms at the far edge of the property.

Although long neglected, the yard retains remnants of earlier times. The tropical fruit trees—*guayaba, mamoncillo, fruta bomba, cherimoya,* and *plátano*—I remember from childhood are still there, although the *vegas de tobacco* Abuelo planted to hand-roll cigars are long gone, as well as my grandmother's roses of various colors. The pungent scent of wet earth rises from the ground. Zoraida takes a deep breath, and her dull eyes scan the high billowing clouds on the horizon above the waving fronds of the distant palms.

Mirta and I wait for her to say something.

Tia inhales again.

"Lo que pasó se entierra aquí," she sighs, and points to the ground.

The past stays buried here.

I don't say what I am thinking: *Just like my grandfather's police revolver and who knows what else.*

She turns away briskly and saunters toward the house. We will never speak of this incident again.

A few days later, before I boarded the taxi waiting at the curb to take me back to Havana for a flight to Washington, D.C., I grabbed an empty plastic film canister from my purse, walked to the yard, and used it to scoop up some dirt.

Zoraida and Mirta watched in silence from the porch as I stuffed the shiny canister into my shoulder bag and waved goodbye as I climbed into the red '57 Chevy taxi for the trip home.

This morning as I sat on a plastic raincoat on a rocky spot near Prajna, I spotted a possible tree for the focus of my meditations. She has wizened branches and is charred and leafless from fire. When I shift my gaze, I glimpse another tree, which brims with shoots and bright, young, tender leaves, its trunk straight and firm. The universe tells me something. The dead tree and the new one are connected by underground invisible threads, an expansive root system that nourishes the field of aspens and the active plant and animal life surrounding me. Life and death are contiguous and interdependent; one cannot exist without another. Existence is composed of endless cycles of past, present, and what is yet to happen—a cha-cha-cha of good with the bad.

I remember the time we tossed my drum teacher's ashes into the Chama

River below, and this ignites a thought. I will do the same with my book when I leave here in a few days. Instead of burying the completed pages, I'll stop at the river's edge at the bottom of the mountain and, in a symbolic gesture, toss them into the gently flowing water. I will watch them drift downstream from the riverbank, swirling past the black stones and branches and brambles on their way to an uncertain destination, just as my grandfather did when he released his caged birds.

Acknowledgments

Many friends, family, and colleagues supported and encouraged the writing of this memoir, especially my husband, David Smith-Soto, who read, offered comments, and advised along the way. I am grateful to my precious daughters, Miranda Arocha Smith and Hilary Borbon Smith, whose keen interest in the Cuban side of our family kept me motivated. My sisters, Olga Cruz and Barbara Arocha Diaz listened to my memories of Cuba and helped fill some critical gaps.

A weekly Zoom call with extended family members that began three years ago during COVID inspired me not to give up the search for a publisher. Many thanks to my former Cuban American colleagues from The Miami Herald--Ileana Oroza, Barbara Gutierrez, Fabiola Santiago, and others, who provided early feedback on several chapters. I am grateful to Guillermo Martinez, my former editor at El Herald, who instructed me on the complexities of Cuban-American politics and taught me how to interview, report, and write *en Cubano*.

The idea for the book emerged over a decade ago when I was a student in the MFA program in Bilingual Creative Writing at the University of Texas El Paso. A heartfelt thanks to Dr. Johnny Payne, former program director, who nearly jumped when I presented the idea for the memoir and exclaimed: "You must write it."

I am deeply grateful to my thesis advisor, Dr. Lex Williford, for his insights into structuring the story and weaving Buddhist elements into the narrative. My good friend, the poet and writer Shelley Armitage, who also served on my thesis committee, provided a close reading of an early version and kept me focused on finding a publisher. Thank you, Shelley, for patiently listening to my family stories. Other UTEP professors who encouraged me along the way include José de Periola, Rosa Alcala, Ben Saenz, Leslie Ullman, Luis Arturo Ramos, Jeff Sirkin, and many others in the Creative Writing department. A close friend, Roger Fidler, a news industry design pioneer, provided valuable suggestions for the cover.

Finishing the book was only possible because of several retreats at Tara Mandala in Southern Colorado. The Tara Mandala sangha sustains and nourishes my life and creative work. I am grateful to Lama Tsultrim Allione, my Tibetan Buddhist teacher, and her husband, David Petit. His death during the first extended retreat on the land inspired me to plumb my past to write about it.

A fellowship at Virginia Center for the Creative Arts in 2022 provided space and time to restructure and rewrite parts of *Guajira*. The Mayborn Conference moved the manuscript forward by awarding it a Literary Excellence Award in 2013.

Thank you, Inlandia Institute for awarding the book your 2022 Eliud Martinez prize and bringing the memoir to readers. Cati Porter, my editor, was insightful and understanding and graciously listened to my ideas for the text and cover. I also appreciate the editing and design work of her Inlandia colleagues Mark Givens and Maria Fernanda Vidaurrazaga.

Y al *pais donde yo naci*, gracias for your gifts of language, culture, and family that abide within.

ABOUT THE AUTHOR

Zita Arocha is an award-winning bilingual writer, journalist, and educator. Born in Cuba and raised in Tampa, she lives in Southern New Mexico. A lifelong advocate for diversity in the news media, she has written extensively about immigration and Latino issues for many publications, including *The Miami Herald* and *The Washington Post*. She is an Emeritus professor of Communication at the University of Texas El Paso, where she taught for two decades and founded the web magazine Borderzine.com. She also earned an MFA in creative writing from UTEP. *Guajira, the Cuba girl*, is her first published book, and she is working on a novel about the Cuban immigrant enclave of Ybor City.

THE AUTHOR IN HAVANA 2009—
PHOTO BY DAVID SMITH-SOTO

About Inlandia Institute

Inlandia Institute is a regional literary non-profit and publishing house. We seek to bring focus to the richness of the literary enterprise that has existed in this region for ages. The mission of the Inlandia Institute is to recognize, support, and expand literary activity in all of its forms in Inland Southern California by publishing books and sponsoring programs that deepen people's awareness, understanding, and appreciation of this unique, complex and creatively vibrant region.

The Institute publishes books, presents free public literary and cultural programming, provides in-school and after school enrichment programs for children and youth, holds free creative writing workshops for teens and adults, and boot camp intensives. In addition, every two years, the Inlandia Institute appoints a distinguished jury panel from outside of the region to name an Inlandia Literary Laureate who serves as an ambassador for the Inlandia Institute, promoting literature, creative literacy, and community. Laureates to date include Susan Straight (2010-2012), Gayle Brandeis (2012-2014), Juan Delgado (2014-2016), Nikia Chaney (2016-2018), and Rachelle Cruz (2018-2020).

To learn more about the Inlandia Institute, please visit our website at www.InlandiaInstitute.org.

INLANDIA BOOKS

Breaking Pattern by Tisha Marie Reichle-Aguilera

Writing from Inlandia annual anthology series

Exit Prohibited by Ellen Estilai

Pretend Plumber by Stephanie Barbé Hammer

Ladybug by Nikia Chaney

Vital: The Future of Healthcare, edited by RM Ambrose

Güero-Güero: The White Mexican and Other Published and Unpublished Stories by Dr. Eliud Martínez

A Short Guide to Finding Your First Home in the United States: An Inlandia anthology on the immigrant experience

Care: Stories by Christopher Records

San Bernardino, Singing, edited by Nikia Chaney

Facing Fire: Art, Wildfire, and the End of Nature in the New West by Douglas McCulloh

In the Sunshine of Neglect: Defining Photographs and Radical Experiments in Inland Southern California,1950 to the Present by Douglas McCulloh

Henry L. A. Jekel: Architect of Eastern Skyscrapers and the California Style by Dr. Vincent Moses and Catherine Whitmore

Orangelandia: The Literature of Inland Citrus edited by Gayle Brandeis

While We're Here We Should Sing by The Why Nots

Go to the Living by Micah Chatterton

No Easy Way: Integrating Riverside Schools - A Victory for Community by Arthur L. Littleworth

About The Eliud Martínez Prize

The Eliud Martínez Prize was established to honor the memory of Eliud Martínez (1935–2020), artist, novelist, and professor emeritus of creative writing at the University of California, Riverside. One prize of $1,000 and book publication through Inlandia Books is awarded annually for a book of fiction or creative nonfiction by a writer who identifies as Hispanic, Latino/a/x, or Chicana/o/x.

Our literary expression occupies a place within our American national literature, and among the literatures of the world.

—Eliud Martínez